# The Laughter of God
## *At Ease with Prayer*

# The Laughter of God
## At Ease with Prayer

by
Miriam Pollard O.C.S.O.

Introduction by
Monika K. Hellwig

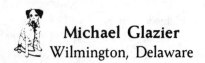

**Michael Glazier**
Wilmington, Delaware

## About the Author

Sister Miriam Pollard is a member of the Cistercian Nuns of the Strict Observance, Mount Saint Mary's Abbey, Wrentham, Massachusetts 02903.

First published in 1986 by Michael Glazier, Inc., 1935 West Fourth Street, Wilmington, Delaware, 19805. ©1986 by Michael Glazier, Inc. All rights reserved. Library of Congress Catalog Card Number: 85-45545. International Standard Book Number: THE LAUGHTER OF GOD: 0-89453-544-7, cloth; 0-89453-549-8, paper. Typography by Debbie L. Farmer. Cover design by Ericka Hellwig. Printed in the United States of America.

# TABLE OF CONTENTS

# INTRODUCTION

This is a book about faith without fear. It is also about faith without frills. In Sister Miriam's conversational and practical style it discusses matters that most of us have not been reading about for quite some time because they have been out of fashion. Distilled out of centuries of monastic life and observance, the book nevertheless presents in a fresh and contemporary way quite relevant to lay readers the pathways into prayer and intimacy with God.

The subject matter is traditional — the types of mental prayer and how to practise them, conversion and the substance of Christian asceticism, examination of conscience and spiritual direction, virtues and so forth. But while the content is traditional, the style is fresh and unique. The examples are perceptive and earthy, and the book comes at a time in which it will be widely useful.

For those familiar with the traditions of Christian spirituality, a particularly refreshing and helpful aspect of these reflections is the author's sober disclaimer of any scheme that might seem to measure progress through degrees of perfection. It is not so much that she is content to leave the measurement entirely to God, as that she finds the whole idea irrelevant if not actually preposterous. And in this she is surely right.

Indeed, the whole book is, in a sense, about the playfulness of God in creation and history — a compassionate and considerate playfulness certainly, but playfulness nonetheless. The essence of play, after all, is that the activity is more important than the goal or product, so that a relationship of love and companionship is always akin to play. In this sense playing and praying are not unlike; they fulfill themselves without having to achieve anything.

This is why the laughter of God, which is mentioned at the beginning of the book, runs silently through it to the end. Sister Miriam's image is that of God laughing *with* us, not *at* us, even when we are not laughing because we do not realize how happy our situation really is when we are so greatly and effectively loved. Faith is, in the last analysis, the opposite of desperation. Tragedy there is aplenty in the world of human affairs, but prayer in faith sees God's love encompassing tragedy. To believe and to persevere in prayer is not to close one's eyes to suffering and injustice and violence, but rather to open one's eyes wider to see all these in the context and perspective of God's redeeming love and welcome.

A book about prayer is never, of course, only about prayer as a separate activity but always also about prayer as transforming the whole of life's experiences and relationships. To pray persistently is to open one's life to the exigence of a holy God. It is at this point that a book about prayer can tend to become forbidding, judgmental, oppressive with its scheme of demands. To approach the matter from the point of view of the playfulness of God does not lessen the demands but it does place them in quite a different light. It removes any sense of a timetable of what must be achieved. Indeed it removes the need to achieve at all, and substitutes the demand to be engaged in the process, to be open to the challenge of the relationship, to be on the way.

To look at Christian asceticism in the context of the laughter and playfulness of God is also to discern and eliminate from that asceticism whatever is contrived, artificial or aimed at demonstrating achievement, no matter how subtly and discreetly.  Athletic competition can have no place in Christian conversion and transformation of life and relationships. The true transformation is simpler, happier and friendlier than that. It is, after all, a matter of allowing God's friendliness and hospitality to prevail over our own insecurity and fear and consequent irritability. It is a matter of learning the art of conversation with fellow creatures, for argument is driven by a purpose beyond itself to persuade, lecture to instruct, admonition to correct, but conversation is its own end — a celebration of fellowship.

Christian conversion and transformation is also a matter of allowing gratitude to prevail in our relationship to God and to fellow creatures. Such gratitude is always expressed in many practical moments, loosely connected, often soon forgotten, interlaced with prayer. Such moments are not stuff for bookkeeping to mark progress or achievement. Indeed, the more lighthearted and self-forgetful they are, the more they are moments of authentic breakthrough. The more they are moments of celebration, and the more they bring healing and peace.

There is an immediacy and simplicity in the practice of spirituality as it is proposed in this book, which is close to the tradition at every point without being bookish or ethereal. It is friendly, earthy and appealing. It is full of common sense in steering a course through the many events that call for our compassion but are not directly subject to our influence. And this is a matter of urgency to most of us in these days of instantaneous mass media communication of war, famine, disaster, oppression, panic and disease. It is all too easy to escape either by putting it all out of one's mind and heart, or by remaining in a constant state of anxiety, ferment and frustration. To be deeply imbued with the playfulness of God who encompasses tragedy with love, is to be wide open in compassion but at peace with one's own limitations in doing anything about the suffering of the world. This is important because true creativity in dealing with the great problems of human suffering is only released within a context of personal serenity.

To appreciate the playfulness of God is to realize that God loves redemptively in the midst of the tragedy, and not only after it is resolved. Rightly understood that does not mean doing nothing to help. It means rather doing the do-able with great confidence and peace of mind, and extending one's compassion without any sense of desperation in the situations that are beyond the do-able.

When all is said and done, the keynote of Christian

spirituality is trust, simplicity and unpretentiousness. These are the qualities by which prayer is woven into the entire texture of life. These are the qualities by which the laughter of God is heard for what it truly is, and by which the playfulness of God awakens a response of authentic human playfulness. This book is a guide to such an approach to Christian spirituality.

*Georgetown University*                    *Monika K. Hellwig*

# FOREWORD

Sometimes I wonder whether God could take us as seriously as we take ourselves. Certainly he is serious. But he is also warm, witty, and ingenious at threading his way among our eccentricities, limitations, and exhibitions of self-interest. He regards with respect our tragedies and our small heroisms, for life is a serious business. It can be painful, and our relationship with God does not dissolve the difficulties. There is no real way to avoid the scrapes and bruises, even sometimes the horrors of human growth. That is not what prayer is for. But it should not add to them, and indeed it should invade our circumstances, pleasant or unpleasant, with a character which I would like to call the humor of God.

Children can be unintentionally entertaining, and when adults laugh, the children are not always pleased. I remember being told, "They're not laughing *at* you; they're laughing *with* you." "But I'm not *laughing!*" God would like to be joined. His humor is not mocking; it does not condescend. It does not dash across our skies like lightning but bubbles up from the mulch on the floor of our daily life. He laughs because he knows more than we do. He has sharper vision. It could be said that he is privy to a secret, except that he himself is the secret of his own laughter.

Our attitude toward God depends on the degree to which we share this secret, and more precisely, on the way in which we perceive the link between God and our daily circumstances. I like the images in which C.S. Lewis evokes our inability to see what is really there. Jill and Eustace, desperate to get out of the storm, struggle without recognition across the very place they are looking for. After the snow, the moors, and the wind, they succeed only in locking themselves away from what they have suffered so much to find.[1] The dwarfs of *The Last Battle*, having arrived at the kind of fragrant heaven an Englishman—or an Anglicized Irishman—would invent, can neither smell the violets nor taste the wine. They have built the stable in which they are trapped, the walls that block the sun, and the trough from which they are sure they must be drinking. "Their prison is only in their own minds, yet they are in that prison. They are so afraid of being taken in that they cannot be taken out."[2] Orual climbs the mountain fighting down a happiness she cannot have on her own terms, and in the moment of revelation, she kneels beside the stream forcing herself to become for the rest of her life a denial of what she knows she has seen.[3]

It would be convenient if we could experience and then hold a clear vision before embarking on our relationship with God, since this relationship is our reason for living at all and

---

[1] C.S. Lewis, *The Silver Chair* (Macmillan NY, 1953).
[2] C.S. Lewis, *The Last Battle* (Macmillan NY, 1956).
[3] C.S. Lewis, *Till We Have Faces* (Eerdmans Grand Rapids, 1956).

what we choose to do with it is what we choose to do with life. But the secret unfolds in the course of the friendship. It cannot be its precondition. We can hesitate to give ourselves to a God we do not know well, someone we have, it would seem, every reason to approach with caution. He can appear as one more burden to carry. He is not. We need to be told he is not. He likes us on bad days—especially on bad days—and he is much more at ease with us than we are with him.

Although the temptation is to enter this uncertain situation a little at a time, I have found by doing it wrong, that having a lot of God is much easier than having a little. Giving a lot to God is much more gracious to the nervous system than giving a little. And by "a lot", I do not mean long hours on one's knees. I mean the readiness to be taken, to be a friend. Portioning out his share is a way of being trapped in our own destructive images of him. The image clears only to the extent of our self-giving, but it can cause complications in the process of the friendship.

I remember the fear and the determination in the eyes of a friend who was very serious about giving herself to God. "Tell me how to do it and I'll do it," she said. I answered, "I think you have. You don't recognize it because you are expecting it to look like something it is not."

She had, and has, three difficulties which many of us share. The image of God which haunts her on an emotional level is one that causes fear. She is giving herself to someone she wants to love but who scares her to death. Secondly, she has an inexact knowledge of the process of self-giving, expecting it to feel as it doesn't and work out in her daily life as it never has. And thirdly, she has never been helped to grasp a number of practical ways in which the project can be chopped into bits small enough to tackle with something like enthusiasm. All she has had to look at is a large formless demand to be very good and a large discouraging experience of not being what she is sure God must want.

If we reflect first on the problem of our image of God, we find that it is generally not our heads that cause the trouble. We know a great deal about God, and if we don't, we should read the right books. What causes the trouble is the effect of life situations on our complex inner worlds. What we know about God can have two aspects—one that is true, and one that is emotionally distorted by what life has done to us. For instance, God is perfection, purifier, lover.

God is perfect. His perfection is an advantage because it means he is reliable. It even means that he is everything we want, but we need time to appreciate that. On the other hand, a perfect person is no fun. He will always be finding fault. The wedding of perfection and imperfection has to be a mismatch. He is too vast and beautiful to take any interest in us, and if he does he will never be satisfied with anything we can do.

It is true that prayer will give us an uncomfortable experience of what we are not, and of what God is. And we will certainly expect of him what we feel this unattractive self deserves. But we also learn that he is not what we expect. He does not spend his time calculating faults. He has better things to do. He is grieved for our sakes when we are slovenly in the pursuit of his friendship, but he is talented enough to turn even our deficiencies to the service of his love. And there is an eventual peace in knowing ourselves valued by him for the persons we really are, a peace which frees us from dependence on the system of evasions and compensations with which we disguise our dislike of the persons we have never wanted to be.

Unfortunately, it's the manner in which we are sure he is going to go about providing these advantages that bothers us—his designs on what the old books called our purification. This also is a truth with two faces. He does make us better. And it's just as well; there is room for improvement. But I think the new books are right to use a different vocabulary. They speak of integration or the process of growth. This climate of thought eliminates the image of a God who prods us with the hot needles of circumstance for the good of our souls. The image of purification can cast us as objects of violence, and turn the spiritual journey into an adventure in nervous apprehension. What is he going to do next?

What he is going to do next is let life happen to us, let some of our dumb choices catch up with us—by no means all. However sour we can become at afflictions we do or do not deserve, we can be certain he has protected us from the maturing of many more unpleasant possibilities than he has permitted to unfold. He is also going to let fall on our heads a storm of benefits so universal that we grow numb to their touch—the satisfactions, joys and common pleasures we no longer bother to feel. He doesn't nail us to a cross. We are better carpenters than he; we do that job ourselves. It is his work to draw out of the wood an abundance of leaf.

To switch metaphors, we could say that although he does not torture, he certainly loves to tinker. The disasters we bring on ourselves, the ones we innocently come by, and the joys of both classes have a twofold nature. They are not added on for the sake of Christian progress. Life won't become terrible because we have brought ourselves to surrender to God. But neither are the circumstances of life impersonal visitations with which he simply helps us cope.

Perhaps I could describe it this way. He dwells inside these commonalities of life. He is a gracious force within what happens to us and what we inflict or bestow on our world. This dynamism is such that it catches up the most anguished and the most inconsequential details of life into a conversation of intricate tenderness. If we give ourselves to this exchange, listening and answering back, we will find our attitudes, our vision, and our capacity for love growing slowly more supple and sure.

I have seen what is called Providence work with such a complexity of patience that it is sometimes hard to "believe in" the existence of God. It is hard to believe in someone whose hands are so obviously shifting around all the furniture of one's life. I have seen him collect a load of incompatible scrap and dump it in a sack. When the bag is found on the back porch of people who least expect it, its yield is not only perfect but perfectly adapted to a desperate need they did not know they had.

He does not afflict us, he changes us. And a life which has had its share of pain becomes easier because it spins off new and gentle meanings, because it has become a person and not a succession of events, a love and not a duty. Oh yes, he is a lover:

> We correctly deny that God has passions; and with us a love that is not passionate means a love that is something less. But the reason why God has no passions is that passions imply passivity and intermission. The passion of love is something that happens to us, as "getting wet" happens to a body; and God is exempt from that "passion" in the same way that water is exempt from "getting wet". He cannot be affected with love, because he *is* love. To imagine that love as something less torrential or less

sharp than our own temporary and derivative "passions" is a most disastrous fantasy.[4]

This however only intensifies our immediate concern. If it is true, he will take away what we now love in order to have us for himself. We want to cry, "Yes, you are bigger and better, but let us keep our little loves. They fit." What if he walks off with what we can't survive losing and leaves us in exchange an admittedly superior presence we have no taste for and lack the capacity to lean on. The substitute gives better value but what good is a more valuable product you can't use, especially when what you have to use it for is as vital a thing as going on with life?

But we've missed the point. We're blaming him for what would have happened anyway, what has to happen if we are to grow, and what is going to happen whether we grow or not. Life itself does things to our loves, our supports and our boltholes. The loves turn yellow around the edges. The projects, careers, people with whom we have identified emotionally slip away or change in such a way that if we are to correspond to what they have become, we must gather resources we are sure we do not have. Our bolt-holes get flooded and we have to dash out into the rain. We can even develop a restless discontent with our contentment. It is not that God has sat up there fulfilling our desires with sawdust. He is down here, moving within the situations that hurt and those that give pleasure, forming our spirits to find their way through the inevitable losses; and the chances are that our capacity for every kind of love will grow. Our hearts will learn to be at

[4]C.S. Lewis, *Miracles* (Macmillan NY, 1947).

home where they had never dreamed to go.

What then of the unspeakable things—the suicide, the overdose, Fr. Ritter's kids, the films from Ethiopia? Would I talk about God's laughter to the nurse still lost in the devastation of her war experience? No, but there are other things I wouldn't talk about either. Anguish is not healed by crushing its victim under the weight of every truth you know. It is healed, or at least assuaged, by listening, by time and acceptance, and often by giving to the other the sense that you also have lived without answers. The silence of God, at first so hard to bear, can become the most satisfying answer, a gracious comfort, the ultimate acceptance. God does not laugh at our pain; his laughter is its resolution.

When Guernsey LePelley retired from the *Christian Science Monitor*, I was grieved. His political cartoons were detached and charitable as well as funny. But more than this, he had given me a genuine spiritual experience, a view of human conflict that was gentle, reverent, and loving. It wasn't in him to despise. His astringent compassion expressed an understanding of turmoil—even of evil—which touched, somewhere beneath its scabby surface, the mystery of its resolution. Not all the truth available to life on earth can be grasped by theological abstraction, but this man, with the delicate instruments of his humor, had probed and expressed what a theologian could not. Or perhaps he is his own kind of theologian. I often felt that if God took his view of our disaster, we had nothing to worry about.

There are other answers of course. We can say there is no God, and this has at least the virtue of indicating that God must be bigger than our apologies for him. Or we can make for ourselves a dreadful God. But faith is more than the refusal to deny the existence of God. It is the willingness to be drawn, at least eventually, from beneath the load placed on us by the God of our own creation. I would like to stick with LePelley, for I think he is closer to the Gospels than he realizes. Often he has dissipated my own turmoil, and I could hear, tumbling out of the silence, out from under the mountain ranges of our guilt, out dissatisfaction, and our boredom, the quick-running stream of the laughter of God.

This is a book that never meant to be one. It was "something about prayer" written for a home prayer group whose members came from various Christian communions or none. It was meant to be an informal guide for people who might be confused by the abundance of material now available on the spiritual life. In fact, it is hard to believe how informal it is. More of a conversation than a book, it does not mean to add but to simplify.

In a limited but practical way, I tried to indicate what surrender to God would look like to a busy person in a very real world, and something of the ways in which the project can be chopped down to a size one can handle. For handling is the point. To mangle Lewis' image a bit, we have to get in and get wet.

Though we should be told the right things about God, life, and ourselves, we do not learn much that way. We learn from the very surrender we want to know all about before embracing it. The vision to live out our surrender develops out of the daily adventure of the ordinary, the moment by moment choice to act as if we saw what is really there. And what is really there is much more satisfactory than what we think we see.

What I wanted most to say is that God is a God of the possible, that the blundering and partial character of our efforts does not surprise or dismay him. It surprises and dismays *us*; he works out the details of the friendship not in spite of, but within and because of our ability to bungle. If our shirts are a bit too stuffed, he is ready to remove some of the padding, and we would do better to smile than to construct a tragedy out of it. He is waiting for us to catch on. He is a God who laughs.

# Part I.

## Prayer, the First Half

# 1

## HOUSE OF THE PASCH

Prayer is sacramental. It is there to begin with. We do not work our way toward it from a distance, or master it as an achievement, like Spanish or cooking. Our task is not to manufacture it but to surrender to the prayer we already possess, to get out of its way:

> For our heart is already in a state of prayer. We receive prayer along with grace in our baptism. The state of grace, as we call it, is, at the level of the heart, a state of prayer. From then on, in the profoundest depths of the self, we have a continuing contact with God. The Holy Spirit takes our heart in tow and turns it toward God. All the time, in fact, he is calling within us and he prays Abba-Father, with supplications and sighs that cannot be put into words, but never for a moment cease within our hearts.

This state of prayer within us is something we always carry about like a hidden treasure. Somewhere our heart is going full pelt, but we do not feel it. We are deaf to our praying heart, we fail to see the light in which we live. For our heart, our true heart, is asleep and it has to be waked gradually—through the course of a whole lifetime.[1]

## Method

The most important part of prayer technique is to keep at it, to give it a daily place in our lives. Even a quarter hour a day is better than a prayer binge now and then. If we are faithful to a daily amount of prayer, we will want to pray at other times during the day, in our various needs and activities. But we must withdraw some time each day from those needs and activities, from the making of our world. Even if the prayer time seems to be no more than a refined nuisance, it is giving life to the rest of our day.

We should give away the time, lay it simply before God without demanding that we see its results. Rabbi Heschel speaks of the Sabbath as a window on eternity. That is what prayer is. We let God in, we let ourselves be the prayer we already are.

Techniques are necessary because we are human and our thoughts get tangled in ourselves—what bothers me, what I have to do, what's going wrong with the people I love, what I want to be, the successful party I gave last night. A simple technique provides a hook on which to hang our wandering

[1] Andre Louf OCSO, *Teach Us How to Pray* (Franciscan Herald Press, *Chicago*, IL 1975.)

concentration. It's not meant to be a straight jacket but a tool. Prayer is like a stream within us, and we are in the habit of letting ourselves and our interests dam up the spring.

The danger with techniques is that we want to use them to accomplish prayer, to get the thing done right. And very often we fall right through our techniques and land with a thump three stories down.

> Technique can put us on the road to prayer, but it cannot of itself bring us to our destination. Techniques have first to grow beyond themselves as it were, exceed themselves in order to be taken up into the Paschal action of Jesus.
> The gulf between a natural technique and the gift of prayer is not to be bridged from man's side. Every technique runs up against the death of Jesus. It is faced with the foolishness of his cross. Through the faith of him who prays, it can be subsumed into the vitalizing dynamic of Easter. Then and only then the gulf is bridged by the grace of the Holy Spirit which is able to turn every technique into a sacrament of Jesus' prayer and of his Pasch.[2]

This is only to warn you not to panic when a useful technique lets you down.

We don't use a method to control God. We don't even use it to control prayer, and if we try we'll find out from experience that it doesn't work.

When it comes to the *amount* of time, of course everyone is too busy. *I'm* too busy. In addition, I'm talking about prayer, not about reading or study. And a beginner, after conversion fervor has been got over, is often embarrassed by want of a substructure on which to base his prayer. He has no history of

[2]Louf.

prayer, at least of this kind, no theological background or scriptural facility. There isn't much to feed his prayer and the time ahead until it can be over looks bleak.

Nevertheless, either half an hour or two blocks of 15 minutes, each seems a good foundation to me, if it can possibly be done without neglecting *real* duty. Often we can survey the day and spot various activities which aren't nearly as important as prayer. Hubert van Zeller, OSB, even suggests that prayer can be a more effective restorative force than many of the things we feel we must have when we are tired—light reading for instance. (Which doesn't mean we should never read novels, but only that since prayer is to our spiritual life as oxygen is to our physical life, one has to dispose of time accordingly.)

Then what about these famous techniques? What type of prayer do we need? How do we learn how?

We go along the road of prayer as we go along the road of any relationship. The whole of us goes. Sometimes we communicate in one way, and sometimes in another. We love in one form, and then in another. And we are simple.

I would suggest a three-part framework whose central section may be varied although even the variations overlap. This is only a very simple way of  making our own, of uniting ourselves with, the great ocean of prayer in the depths of our hearts.

The first form we will put into the center is wordless (almost) and imageless. It is contemplative in nature, and is very basic to the needs of man. You find something like it in many traditions.

## 1. THE ANTECHAMBER

This may well be the most important part. Keith Clark, OFM Cap, speaks of his sacred place. He found a tree or even set a blanket on the floor, and by that symbol he entered a sacred space.[3] It's not that the rest of our life isn't also sacred. It's that when we come to pray in this manner, we have to change our way of being present to the world, to ourselves, to God. When we are in the midst of an active life, we love in an active way, we grasp reality and deal with it, we practice virtue. This is good though it can tend in the Western temperament to become too exclusively active. In addition, we all have a number of emotional tugs and knots. We have to let God transpose our physical and psychological being into another key. We need a framework of quiet, receptivity. And

When using this image I am reminded of Marcel Breuer's magnificent church at Collegeville, Minnesota. We enter the church through an enclosed version of the atrium or forecourt, customary in older churches. In a modern adaptation of traditional practice, he has placed the baptismal area here, recessed into the floor and resembling the font of immersion with its symbolism of descent into the waters of Christ's death and emergence into the glory of his resurrected life. The only light enters from glass panels directly above the font; the baptismal area is surrounded by growing plants; and the holy water vessels stand at its four corners. We enter the church

[3]Keith Clark OFM Cap, *Make Space, Make Symbols* (Ave Maria Press, Notre Dame IN, 1979).

seem to make impossible the state of quiet we have determined we need for prayer. Generally, two factors are involved here.

The first is that once we have done a certain responsible amount to dispose our lives toward God and make them available to his work in them, we must let go. He takes us at our word—he takes over. If we were to have control of our lives, if we were able to arrange them according to our ideas of what must be necessary to please God, we would wind up as prayerful and independent masters. God couldn't get *in*. We would be "praying," but we would be walled away from God.

The second reason is that as we grow, basic emotional areas have to be invaded and exposed in order to be given to God and also healed. This causes pain, upset, tension. I am very calm and peaceful when my self-image isn't threatened. My prayer chugs along beautifully when I am accomplishing creative projects, when I experience myself as affirmed, when I stand guard over a small area of superior ability which I've staked out for myself. The inspirations are glorious. When I have failed, when I've shown myself as poised as a two-legged stool, as loving as a closed and bolted door, I'm upset. My prayer is difficult. I resent God. Sometimes I am so upset I want to put off the prayer until I can do a better job. I wonder whether there is a more destructive temptation.

I'm not *there* to do a good job, I'm there to be invaded by a love that demands that I open these cramped corners of myself to its healing so that I can yield myself more and more deeply, so that I can begin really to be the wonderful gift he has placed inside me. The people who are difficult to love, the frustrating demands when I have something to accomplish, the flops when I want to succeed, arouse emotional responses which tell me things I need to know about myself; they open areas I would like to keep closed. Oddly, it is often at times of emotional disturbance, when our whole being is concentrated on some object of our enflamed emotions, that we most should pray. It won't be a neat prayer. We probably couldn't achieve a calm and "deep" form of consciousness. But we are out of our Sunday clothes, and our areas of need are bare and unadorned. At this point, our prayer is probably an invitation to God to come into those depths, those dark and hurting places. We are willing to be known, touched, even changed. We ask the grace to let go of whatever selfishness is being manifested in this way.

We will hurt also when we move out of security and try to stop setting up our world for the purpose of our own protection and advancement. We will be upset in the very pursuit of virtue, because uncramping hands which have clutched in one way or another, being firm when it is easier to be liked, undertaking tiresome duties when some pleasure is far more attractive can all cause psychological disturbance. If moving out of ourselves "disturbs" our prayer, we shouldn't worry. Moving out of ourselves is more important than calm at prayer.

What will happen, in some way, is that the prayer will help us in our journey outward. The pain of uncurling from around ourselves can be woven into prayer where, in ways not usually apparent to us, it is supported and pushed into constructive channels. But this is not really our business.

One thing to keep in mind is that though we need other prayer forms in addition to this one, do for instance need to through our baptism. Our prayer, our community, our worship, our life and our joy emerge from the gift of faith consummated in baptism.

That's what our little prayer vestibule is also. It is a passing through baptism, a deepening entry into it. The prayer atrium is Paschal. And somehow it should contain the primary Paschal qualities. It should be:

*Positive*, a recognition of what we are in Christ. We may feel dry or deflated. We may be suffering. But even the suffering Christian has the privilege of being enfolded in the great suffering One.

*Dependent*. We aren't putting on a performance, building a house, or passing an exam. We are only trying to keep our managing-selves from damming up the stream. We want to let God make us receptive, the person we most deeply are, there where his prayer bubbles up out of the source of our life.

*Personal*. Again, prayer isn't a thing or a performance but a personal presence and love.

Just how we go about building our vestibule or anteroom depends on temperament, situation, emotional or physical state at the moment. Here are some suggestions.

Some people can find a sacred place—a corner of backyard, an empty room or a piece of attic, even a window where the seasons go by. A special chair, a special time of day. Keith Clark wound up with his blanket and candle. For some, a single symbolic object can create its own space—a candle, a cross or a crucifix, a reproduction of Mondrian or Rembrandt, an icon, an empty basket, a simple vase arrangement before a bare piece of wall, a desk top in bare state (*some* people are that way). If we *know* it has to be 15 minutes or half an hour, we won't be itching to get away.

Sometimes an interior symbol can help. I find it helpful to imagine myself opening a door—either to a small room or to a walled garden. I put in the key or lift the latch, open the door, step in, close the door, latch it behind me and walk slowly to a place inside. This is not imaginative embellishment. Our natural links with all these primary symbols are invoked and drawn into prayer. Often, we are stopped by one, and linger there. For today or for 10 minutes of today, all our prayer is the quiet attitude of setting a key in a lock and turning it, or of opening a door. Some days, we can stop simply at the mystery of a room beyond and of our reluctance to enter. We can let the reluctance open itself to the otherness or the invasiveness or the threat of what we are afraid to enter. A threshold says to us without words and concepts many basic human things with which we have a need to be in tune.

For some, a quiet slow decade of the rosary forms an anteroom. Or the Our Father. If we find ourselves tense, we may realize that this tension is telling us something about ourselves. Am I angry at my circumstances? Do I feel unloved by someone I deeply cherish? Perhaps the best prayer-atrium is a long frank gaze at what bothers me and an enfolding of it in the redeeming gentleness of Merlin Carothers' prayer of praise[4] which is a contemporary, very positive form of the classical prayer of abandonment and trust.

Breathing rhythmically and deeply can be more than a form of relaxation. An ancient tradition uses the indrawn breath to give over our entire being to the presence and power of the

[4]Merlin R. Carothers, *Prison to Praise* (Logos International, 1970). Other Praise books available: Foundation of Praise, Inc. Box 1430, Escondido, CA 92025.

Spirit, drawing him as it were into every area of ourselves. Then the outpoured breath is the Spirit—permeated prayer, the gift of oneself borne on the Spirit as he pours himself out into the Trinity.

Often there is no sharp line between the antechamber and the prayer at the center. And if part of the preliminary presence becomes a still pool of prayer, stay there. We mustn't think "this is five minutes of *this*. Now, on to the real thing." The vestibule is prayer in itself. It is very important because often we give up on prayer when it doesn't conform to our expectations. And if we have done this much (created or let God create a vestibule) we have opened our hands and put them in God's. The result is his affair. We hope we will have calmed down, but we shouldn't be discouraged if our life has provided us with a good deal of interior jangle. We have given a little shape to our prayer time, made a kind of bowl for him to fill. *How* he fills it will not always please us, but that is really not why we're praying.

## 2. THE QUIET PRAYER

After passing through our vestibule, we enter a prayer which does not picture things or speak or reason about divine truths or pour out feelings or resolutions. It is present to God. It is there, with him. It rests on the immense intimacy of his presence in our own heart. We are turned to him, immersed in him. We are content to be, and to be his.

This prayer has various forms, because it is too hard for us to keep our minds still and given in that way. The form helps.

The Jesus prayer. This prayer uses the cry of the blind man

on the Jericho road: "Jesus son of David, have mercy on me." But it changes the address in order to address the risen Lord of Glory: "Lord Jesus Christ, have mercy on me." Often this is combined with the breathing mentioned before, the address on the in-drawn breath, the petition on the outward. It is not meant to be a rumination on our sinfulness or a meditation on salvation. It is a simple, quiet, rhythmic way of situating ourselves in our real relation to God, in the glorious tenderness of his mercy. We stay there. We are the person his mercy is creating. We accept to be this.

Sometimes the word is shortened to the name of Jesus. It is not merely an address. The name is a healing power, a loving presence. We draw it down into our deepest self and let it seep through all our darkness. Again, we simply *are*, holding the name in ourselves, absorbed in the person it holds. The name to a Semite was not a label but a presence of the one named. We do not have to say it constantly, but only renew its presence when our attention wanders. Or again, it can be combined with breathing.

Basil Pennington OCSO has popularized what he calls Centering Prayer, a form of this type, a simple presence in which some sacred word, or a few, are used as a focus to which we return when we have wandered off. It differs from Eastern mantras in its orientation. A word for us is full and personal and living. You can't use the word Jesus, or Lord, or mercy, or grace without clothing yourself in a personal relationship, without placing yourself in the stream of a personal salvation. Here again the object of this prayer is God, personal presence to the living prayer within us. We turn gently to our word when our attention is taken by ourselves or by lovely thoughts however holy, for we want to remain in that place within ourselves which is too full to have yet become thought.

We can use our icon as another form. We can sit before it in receptivity, not reasoning anything out, not offering our feelings, not generating acts of love, simply being in the presence of whatever it offers us—mystery, say, or tenderness, or gentleness or majesty. Listen with your eyes until it says one thing and then rest in that. Transcendence often. Concern. Simply a revelation of what he is.

Obviously, we don't approach these forms like a bargain counter, a little of each in one sitting. Otherwise, handle the method easily and as it seems best for you, remaining faithfully with it, being flexible to its needs, but realizing it is not a mechanical means to "success in prayer." You aren't praying in order to succeed.


## 3. THE RETURN

This is also a transition, and to be honest, I always neglect it but the reasons for being faithful to it are excellent. Physically, psychologically, we have gentled-down, assumed toward ourselves and what is not ourselves an attitude which differs very much from the way we usually respond to the demands of an active life. If we've managed to pray, and the time is up, we're tempted to hop up and rush back to these demands, or (if we've liked the prayer) heave ourselves back with reluctance.

We hope that eventually these periods of prayer will more and more invade our attitudes toward active daily living, that we will become more balanced and integrated, the receptive and gentle in us responding to challenge, irritation, fatigue, frustration, creative accomplishment. We hope that we will meet in our daily world the God we have met in quiet, that our activity will not lose its verve but take on added depth.

However, there will always be a transition. Even in a culture more respectful of silence and receptivity than ours, human beings need to pass from one mode of being to another, and they need a graceful means of passage. So we take a few minutes at the end of the prayer to accept anew the call to our daily vocation. Perhaps a slow and simple Our Father or a small vocal prayer we compose on the spot will do it. We should look out into the world before stepping back into it, and ask for it to be touched with prayer. The same great mystery which lives in our deepest heart is calling to us from the world around us, in our daily duties, our family, work, in the needs and delights of an ordinary day. We say yes, but we say it with perhaps less frenzy, and we ask that we may be less inclined to pounce on our tasks as something to be accomplished or a battle to be won, or a job to be checked off the list, and more inclined to open ourselves to them as encounters with a living presence, and abiding love. We reconsecrate ourselves to the world, we let the morning's (or whenever it is) prayer anoint our day with the passion and resurrection of Christ.

Perhaps we have a favorite passage from Scripture or another book which will help us to go back in this way. Or perhaps we could assemble a small collection of *short* helpful texts of this nature.

What I have called quiet prayer, and inserted first into our framework is flexible, adaptable, simple. It should form part of our prayer life because we need it, but it should not be the whole. There is no rule about how often to devote our daily time to this form. We just should get it in as a part of our whole prayer scheme. Sometimes we might like a week or two of just this, sometimes vary it with other forms, sometimes let the other forms predominate.

The interesting thing is that this type of prayer is going to take an increasingly large place in the other forms as well. It easily slips in when we are praying in a *lectio* form, as well as in what I am going to call the prayer of emotional honesty. It's a natural way of being-with, and there's no great point in making air-tight categories. We might start out with another form and wind up here.

Some things to watch out for:

If we feel that imageless and wordless prayer is the most advanced prayer, we will regard it as big league stuff, and consequently all other kinds of prayer as stepping stones to be passed over. This is a shame, because it's using a *form* of prayer as a crutch for the self-image, and obstructing the purpose of prayer.

Another temptation is to undervalue the humanity of Christ. It is possible to regard the humanity as a bridge to the divinity, a stage in the relationship with God which is to be transcended in one's ascent to a purer state. But God doesn't take this view. The Word has not discarded the human nature of Christ, and it is in the whole Christ that we share the life of the Trinity.

Our prayer and our relationship with God do become simpler (if we let them) in the course of growth. Prayer can be entertaining at first. We can enjoy picturing biblical scenes or thinking rationally about divine truths. We may have the support of emotional love for God. Later, the prayer will find itself on a small rock island, dry and dissatisfied, our emotions unpampered. We can't entertain ourselves anymore. The prayer becomes a kind of waiting in faith and patience.

But this is not the same thing as identifying a *form* of prayer (which in itself can be used by beginners) with an advanced stage of prayer. And one of the holiest, most brilliant monks in the world, in the course of a conference on prayer recently, told us "your imagination has been consecrated. It is holy. Use it. Use the Gospels to know Jesus. It is all in that—know Jesus." He has one of the most extraordinary minds God ever made, but he is also too simple to care what stage of prayer he's at.

I've seen a quiet prayer-form desired and pursued as an end in itself. It can be called "deep prayer" as if it were more valuable than any other. People can try to set up a life-style (or escape from an uncongenial one) in order to obtain an atmosphere of peace, tranquility, and quiet. They can pursue the quiet *state* of prayer as if that were the good to be obtained and not the union of one's whole self with God—or as if the quiet state automatically assures that union. This is very dangerous. It is true many modern life-styles are crazy, that a prudent person would do well to consider what improvements can be made to minimize selfishness and maintain better balance. But no matter how prudent we are, many upsetting elements are willed by God. However much we may justly try to bring our emotional attitudes from violence to gentleness, an unruffled sea is not ideal.

Often we are placed in very upsetting circumstances. Often the demands of our vocation or our God-given relationships talk to God about ourselves, we shouldn't abandon this form entirely because it is difficult. The mere position of being turned wholly to God is healing and helpful—the attitude of suspending our worries and waiting gently on a far greater reality and a love which is their solution. It's also a good tonic for people who want to solve all their problems by figuring them out.

# 2

# ALTERNATIVES

Since the central section of our prayer form need not always be what I have called quiet prayer, I will describe two other kinds which might be used instead.

## The Prayer of Emotional Honesty

This type of prayer might be called any number of things or not have a title, but titles are handy, so we will call it the prayer of emotional honesty.

It has the same three elements. I'm more and more convinced that in this time we set aside for prayer, we shouldn't just throw ourselves in (and drag ourselves out) any old way. Some people, and all people sometimes, require very little anteroom, but at least a little one should be there. Sometimes it is the whole of the prayer time, and the loving acceptance of not being able to go further is the whole prayer. At other times of the day, diving-in will be possible because at *this* time we passed through our vestibule. This period of prayer is the root of the rest of the day's prayer and presence to God.

The point of the anteroom is not to get ourselves spruced up for God and to put on company manners. It is to let ourselves be taken by the hand and pulled very gently out of the ruts of activity and pose into which we slip and which fit so tightly we are in danger of cramming our prayer into the same pattern. It is also a way of realizing what the reality of life is—not something I construct but something I am given. And it is a way of being very simple with God.

Therefore we have first our anteroom, then the main part of the prayer, which is something like this:

You know how it is with someone you love deeply and with whom you have a very close relationship. You are willing to be known. It's not just your political opinions or your evaluations of how your career is going that you share. It's not just the values on which you base your choices or the things you like to do and read, though all this has a part in the offering of yourself. It's the opening of your feelings that creates the intimacy of your love. You give your whole self, not simply the part of yourself which reasons and evaluates. You are willing to be known, not simply as the person your mind and skill have created to face the world, but as a very basic self who fears, is jealous or resentful or angry or ambitious, weak or troubled, happy or puzzled.

With God, we have the sense of "well, he wants us to be good," which is true enough, but we don't always realize how. We feel that prayer is the place to pull our disordered self together, give ourselves a sermon on how we should live and the kind of person we should be, make excellent resolutions, dispose ourselves for the blessing of God upon our efforts, and ride off so fortified into renewed combat. I don't see how anyone can persevere in prayer that way.

Have you ever tried to relate to people who can't share themselves emotionally? They can be very good, but it drives you crazy, because you can never enter their doubts, their disappointments, their fear or pleasure or despair. You sit with your back against a stone wall. You could go to them for any amount of help. They will give themselves generously, listen to you, be loyal to you. They can't give themselves to personal intimacy because they can't let anyone into their emotional life. Maybe they've been brought up to believe they shouldn't have one.

That's what we do to God when we lock him out of our feelings. What he wants of us is pretty much what *we* would want of a good human relationship. He wants to share all of us, all the way down.

How to go about this is not always apparent. I used to write it down, almost as a letter to God (and then destroy it after awhile—it wasn't a diary, it was prayer, and had served its purpose). Or we can quietly bring up one area of ourselves—a precious relationship, a job problem, a difficulty in learning or succeeding. We can tell God about it and intersperse our telling with periods of silence. Perhaps he wants to tell us something about it too, if not at this time, then at least some other time when a little opening will come.

If we are angry at God, we ought to tell him so. We can say what we please. He understands.

One effect of this is simply that we are more given, more open. Another effect is that we come to understand from experience that God loves and accepts us as emotional beings. Emotions aren't wrong. It's our acts and our choices that involve morality—how we choose to handle the feelings. If I'm angry, I should tell God, not keep trying to feel the right way in order to pray. I should not either go off and give my husband a black eye. By laying my heart open to God (and by getting help if I need it with a communication problem with my husband; or by getting help to deal with a bad marriage) I can find some way to turn my destructive emotion into something else. I shouldn't oversimplify here. A deeply rooted problem needs help. I can't offer prayer as a substitute for counsel when this is needed. But I doubt that any help will do all it can *without* prayer.

Realizing how much God loves us *as* emotional beings can change our whole relationship to him. We will *go* to him when we feel awful. We won't stay away because he couldn't approve us until we feel all the correct things. If we're "too tired to pray," we will know that it's important for him to share the fatigue, to know we want to bring it to him, that he cares and wants us with him. If something beautiful happens and we can't wait to share it with someone we love, we'll go to him first because our joy is important to him — more, to share *us* in our joy is important to him. If we are confused, puzzled, doubtful, we will share it with him. Whether we get answers or not, because the confusion and doubt are part of us, and he wants all of us.

One more thing will happen, the biggest of all. Just as our reason and our making-faculties are not all of us, so too our emotions are not all of us. When we bring our whole self to prayer, that self becomes rooted more and more deeply in our baptismal grace, in all the divine gifts which make us partakers in the life of God. And so our emotions too sink roots deeply into the soil for which they were made, God's own life, and our fragmented natures grow into greater harmony. *All-of-us* is a thing much greater than any or all of our human faculties. All-of-us is a beautiful harmony of human and divine. We don't dump our emotions somewhere on the way to heaven. They, like the rest of what makes us up, have to grow, to enter more and more deeply into love. Sometimes it will feel as if they are being pulled out by the roots or stomped on, but they will be with us forever, our glorious companions for eternity, permeated with divine life as the leaves are with sunlight. They will not be destroyed; they will be raised to what they were destined from our birth to be—glorious and grateful roads on which God has walked, and even more, even closer than that, for he enters and possesses them and suffuses them with himself.

The third part, as with the first type of prayer, is the return. We haven't abandoned the world that disturbed or excited or tempted or bewildered us. For a little while we have shared with God the self which that world has affected. Perhaps at the end, we could be grateful. And ask the strength to find him there, to find him in whatever distresses or delights us, as he moves in everything that touches us to deepen and form us to his friendship.

One other form of this prayer can be mentioned here, although it will be gone into later in more detail. Obviously, we will spend our lives—or a good deal of them—handling emotions in such a way that they are brought into the service of virtue and a deepening love. We have to recognize them (often dimly) first, then expose them gently to God, then work out simple ways of nudging them into channels where they will be of assistance to faith and reason, where they will be servants and not masters.

This project too is material for prayer. And as in all moral endeavor, the big, vague, global view is not profitable. "I'm so proud." (Indeed, you have lots of company.) Neither does it help to spend half an hour beating oneself over the head for every possible evil in one's soul. What does help is trying to recognize very concrete, down-to-earth manifestations of some dominant tendency. "I am very critical of others because it makes me feel superior, because I can do it with wit and get a laugh, because I can revel in a talent for psychological appraisal." And what this signifies on a deeper level, you don't know yet.

This specific thing you open to God. You quietly set it in his hands, you do so lovingly, knowing he accepts the you which you are giving. You don't force. You ask for the help you need to grasp and work on the situation. Little by little you will see more, but the main point of this prayer is to sink your fault into the loving death and resurrection of Christ, to release it from the limitations of the merely human so that your struggle to turn it into a constructive avenue for love will become itself a loving, divine enterprise.

As the project goes on, more light comes, but the purpose of this prayer is not to provide an introspective binge, or an opportunity to get yourself so intensively programmed for virtue that the whole thing ceases to be a relationship and becomes a process. You make a simple resolution—the simpler the better—after opening yourself to God. You place it in his hands, and review it gently in his presence maybe twice a day—no more. "When I realize I have been critical, or when I am bathing myself happily in critical thoughts, I will praise God for this person exactly as he is, and ask God for the light to see that this person just as he is, is exactly what I need." If I am faithful, if I return to God at regular intervals with this prayer, he will guide my growth. The big thing to realize is that we do not wait *until* we are better (to be in better shape for facing God) to pray. We pray first and we keep praying during the getting-better. And especially when it seems we are not getting better. For one thing, we will never get better enough to face God. We never can take a stand on our goodness. We always take a stand on our need. All our goodness is his gift. I am an emptiness which delights in being filled, and which he delights in filling. If I don't go to him in prayer, I will not *get* better.

Louis Evely tells a beautiful story about one of his students who could not quit smoking. The boy felt he was chained to his habit and wanted to be free. He had given it up over and over and never succeeded. (Those were the days when kids only smoked tobbacco, but he couldn't kick even that.) He came to tell Evely he was giving it up (again) for Lent. Evely told him he was sick of the program. "On the contrary, you will smoke for Lent." After three weeks, the boy came back. "I don't smoke any more." In the course of trying to smoke to please God, he had recognized in his smoking not pleasure but rebellion. Once he had forced himself to imagine God offering him a cigarette and enjoying his enjoyment, he no longer wanted or needed the cigarette. It would have been an intrusion on the moments of intimacy shared with this close and tender God.[5]

It's sort of like that with prayer and moral effort. Moral effort doesn't prepare us for God. God prepares us for moral effort. Then as we accept and use the gifts of grace with which he supplies us, he draws us on further and gives us what we need to answer his new lights and demands.

But watch it — he is not nearly so interested in the perfect product as we are. (And we will come back to this.) He wants our striving, and our openness in sharing the striving. He wants the relationship which grows out of the striving. But when we pray in this way, we must let go of what *we* want ourselves to become, or we will stop praying when we don't get what we want — and we won't. Do what you know *he* wants, and know that as long as you keep trying and praying, all is well.

## Lectio Divina

Another alternative for our mid-section of the framework is the primary monastic prayer, *Lectio Divina*. It is a prayer form, not a kind of reading. It is very different from any kind of reading we are used to. It is so flexible that it can take in the previous two forms of prayer and a few more besides.

[5]Louis Evely, *Suffering* (Herder, NY, 1967)

We begin with our famous vestibule, and then into it we introduce the word of God.

What to use? We *can* use non-Biblical sources. If you have a favorite book which is easy to pray over, this can be used—a section of it which is already familiar to you, so you won't be agitated with getting on with it. But for every time you use a non-Biblical source, I would recommend using the Bible four to five times. And if you almost always use the Bible, that is fine. A liturgical text such as the Holy Saturday celebration of the New Fire is also good. The marriage ceremony.

I would use the Gospels at least once a week, even if you are "doing" an Epistle. And go back to the Gospels for a few weeks in between Epistles (or Acts, or the Old Testament). Don't lose your immediate contact with the personality of Jesus in the Gospels.

This prayer form should be everyone's staple diet, the core of his prayer life, primarily because we need the nourishment of God's Word. It is food and light. It is not a thing but a living person. It is a presence of God which acts in our minds, hearts, wills. We need it, and we need to receive it prayerfully.

The main part of the prayer consists of a relationship between ourselves and God as he is offering himself to us in his word.

> The Word that I am turning over in my heart is, after all, no merely human word without life or lustre. It is God's word; that is to say it is a seed of life that can strike root and germinate; it is a glowing coal that purifies and gives warmth. Of course we must take care not to wander off into an intellectual analysis of some truth or other concerning God. We are standing here at the very base, the very springs of our heart and of our existence, with our defenses down, exposed to the love of God, to the

power of the Spirit and to the consuming omnipotence of his Word.

I dwell upon it, stand guard over it, I take it over and repeat it slowly in the silence of my heart. I rock it to and fro in this interior region of myself. I ruminate upon it, chew it over. I let it soak right into my heart. It amounts, quite literally, to a flushing out of the heart.[6]

Ambrose Southey, OCSO, our Abbot General, gave us a very simple and beautiful conference on the practice of this prayer. He took as his text the gospel story of the mother of James and John requesting of Jesus that her sons receive the best seats in the Kingdom. Any text with possibilities can be used—a parable, a sentence, a phrase. You may want to choose a text from a part of the Bible which you are currently studying (out of prayer time—I mean the study is) so that its meaning and symbolism are apparent to you. "Available" to you is a better word—you have a good grasp of what the sacred author meant to say. But you do not go off into analysis. You treat it very simply. I can't give an exact transcription of the Abbot General's talk, but this is an account of it as it has become mine, as they say, through the years:

I look at the story. What strikes me as I read it slowly is that people whom Jesus was instructing manifest a complete lack of understanding and a gross violation of the values he was trying to impart. And how does he react? I rest in the gentle acceptance of his reaction. Personal hurt does not strike back. He does not take a position above them and throw down a castigation they could not grasp at this time. He questions, he treats them with courtesy and respect. He sees them as they

[6]Louf.

will someday be, and he draws them along the way to that
someday in a measure they can grapple with at this stage of
their growth. I look at his reaction slowly, at his method of
teaching and relating to those over whom he is placed. I let
him enter my heart in this moment of his self-revelation. I am
quiet. I listen and watch. I ask myself how I react in a similar
position, with those I am called to teach and guide. I immerse
my own efforts in this moment of Jesus.

Or, the Abbot said, perhaps at another time. I am drawn to
throw upon this scene the light of other scriptural passages.
Slowly I say against this background the Beatitudes of Mat-
thew. Or I remember the two thieves, one on his left and one
on his right. "Lord, remember me when you come into your
kingdom." I let the word Kingdom rest gently within me. "My
cup you will indeed drink," and I am drawn to the Garden, to
the cup of my own life . . .

Another prayer time, I may be content merely to ruminate
the word "Glory." I use it as the medium of my awareness of
Jesus. I rest in it and so in him, saying it slowly as a kind of
touch. I let myself be drawn into adoration, very still.

Or, I may use a psalm, going through it very slowly, with
pauses into which the words can fall like seeds.

I can identify with one person or another, see whom I feel
most like and why. I can use the attitude of someone else to
carry my own to God—Peter's tears, Magdalen's joy in the
Garden, Paul's enthusiasm.

Scripture is an enormous country and I am free to walk
there. Not in discursive reasoning—that has its place, but not
here. Here we wind down, we are listeners, watchers. We
leave silences as space to give us room to uncramp.

One thing I did during Lent was to take each character in Mark's scene of Jesus with Pilate and study it, taking my time, drawing as much as possible out of each. For instance, Jesus: the principle characteristic of Jesus in this scene is silence. All the synoptics emphasize it. The Greek text is very strong—two sets of double negatives. You ask yourself about this. Why? What was the character of his silence? What does Mark wish it to mean? I checked the commentary of Wilfrid Harrington, OP[7] (but not at prayer time), then confronted the text. Was Jesus emotionally undisturbed? Despairing? Disdainful? I remembered a conference of Jean LeClerq OSB, who told us that this silence of Jesus is the paradigm, the primordial sacrament of any religious silence we undertake ourselves, that it was not an emptiness but a fullness. You can then simply rest in this mystery of wordlessness. You can try to absorb it into yourself, make place in your heart for it.

And so with the other characters—Barabbas, the crowd, Pilate, the priests.

Obviously, this prayer form can become at any time either of the forms previously mentioned. It can run naturally into quiet prayer, holding a single word or phrase in its heart. Or our confrontation with the text, our setting of ourselves within the text, can uncover emotional situations which we must be honest about with God. *Lectio* seems to me the richest prayer form, because it can include the others and because it increases our knowledge of God through encounter with his word. He enters our heart as his own explanation. We are taking in food for mind and heart. God has willed to make

---

[7] Wilfrid Harrington, OP, *Mark*: Vol 4 of New Testament Message (Michael Glazier, Wilmington DE, 1979).

himself known to us in his word. It is part of his incarnation, and part of his incarnation in us.

This is the place to mention that we can always use a small passage of Scripture in our anteroom period. Sometimes I come in from a morning of everything going wrong, or at least of being tired and keyed up, and *know* I can't pray. I take a little bit of Scripture and put it down gently into the interior chaos as a healing power, a presence that will bring meaning out of a day on which it seems a mistake to have gotten up. Whether or not you *feel* relief, the word has been given an opening. It is going to work, setting about its task.

## Spill-Over

This half hour is obviously not the extent of our prayer life. It is meant to be a root, a kind of spring from which our daily attitudes and our presence to God will flow. We use other types of prayer all day long.

If we are living Merlin Carothers' praise spirituality, our day will be a tissue of prayer as we meet each new element with praise, believing in it as a touch of love.

There are the little prayers for help when we are disorganized and oppressed, the moments of weariness when we draw some good deep breaths and dip ourselves in the prayer-word or text of today's prayer session.

Times when we have to wait—at checkout counters, traffic lights, customers to be waited on. When we're eating alone. Before we begin something—a class, a morning's work, the making of a meal—to consecrate it, to see in it and our own contribution to it the hands of the risen and glorious Lord remaking his creation as a gift to the Father.

Times when we have only a few moments to listen and be aware of the infinite prayer within us, the ocean of prayer on which we are borne. When we feel impotent and dry, we know we possess the prayer of Jesus in Gethsemani, on the cross, on Resurrection morning, the prayer of healing and blessing with which he welcomed all the prosaic details of his ordinary life. We can rest in this and offer it as our own prayer. It is our own relationship to God.

There are infinite ways of using a prayer list. It can even on occasion form one's daily half-hour.

1. Praise God for all the beauty in the person, for all the defects, suffering, and moral lapses of his life. Praise God because all the inadequate and painful elements we see are hiding places for the loving work of God, bringing this member of Christ's body to happiness and goodness in a way we *can't* see. This is a very restful prayer.

2. Sink into God's love for the other, who is enfolded in this horizonless, infinite love. Love this person with God's own love.

3. Place yourself within the person, in quiet attentiveness before God. Ask healing and opening from within the other's need.

4. Ask God how you may improve your relationship with this person. Ask forgiveness for anything you have done to spoil it.

This kind of thing—one of the above, not all, and relating to a single person—can occupy an idle moment. You'd be surprised how many little chinks in the day can be filled with restful prayer. Not trying to cram as many prayers into a day as you can, but reaching out gently to touch the hand of God, or simply to be aware of his presence. A few slow deep breaths, the Jesus prayer.

There is also what could be called acted prayer. As a procession or a pilgrimage is a form of prayer, both being symbols of the Paschal journey which is our life, so can a great many other things be made into acted prayer. Remember Keith Clark's small journey in search of a sacred place? Doing the dishes can be. Taking a shower if we aren't in such a blamed hurry to get it over with. Visiting a shut-in, clipping the hedge. You can be sure, sure, sure you have no time after your half hour and then question yourself about what is rattling through your head during these daily manual tasks. All you need to do (all!) is realize what you're doing, be present to it instead of getting it over with.

Unpleasant things can become acted prayers, the acting out of my surrender to God and to the loving service of his people. Thinking of it like this redeems it from the pain-in-the-neck category and even from the offer-it-up category which doesn't help some of us much.

Beautiful things can be done this way, and prepared for. If you're going to a wedding, you can spend several daily prayer times on its symbolism. You're not going just to watch a ceremony but to take part in the celebration of a sacrament. A sacrament is churchly, and so are you. It's not "their" wedding. It's an acting out of the incarnation of the Word, the union of God and man in Christ Jesus. It's a re-entry, a confirmation of your own marriage as a participation in this bridal union of God and man, an opportunity to renew your oneness with this couple and the whole world in Christ.

Receiving and enjoying a letter can be this. You can establish a small vestibule, a loving silence, open to God. Then you can read the letter knowing that God's love is coming to you in the loving friendship you are sharing. He has extended his kingdom in the world a little more because of the joy of the sharing. Then a gentle communion with him in gratitude when you are done.

This kind of thing is not a substitute for the daily half-hour. It is the fruit of it.

The rosary is also beautiful and can be very contemplative. Romano Guardini calls it a sacred place. You mustn't rush to get it in though. A decade with pauses and in a relaxed manner is better than a rushed whole. The aim is not to get a prayer said as if in itself this were an accomplishment, but to be quietly united to God. The prayers of the rosary are only a medium for contemplation, like the murmur of trees or sea. They introduce us into a gentler rhythm where we can simply be present to the mysteries. Stations of the Cross can be a profound prayer. You don't have to finish them if a slower pace is more natural. Maybe do the rest at other times.

The trouble with the Stations is that we often don't have enought Scriptural background to appreciate what the Evangelists are telling us in the Passion narrative, so our praying of the Stations can be either empty or sentimental. Often we need lectio as well as study of the Passion narratives as a way of growing into the Stations.

Which brings us to what I am going to call the other half of prayer.

# Part II.

## Prayer, the Other Half

# 3

# A BOOK FOR THE HAND

Prayer in itself is not enough. It's obvious that the moral life must feed us, not always obvious that we need intellectual feeding as well. Our prayer needs background.

## Study

First, because it's easier, we'll talk about formation of the mind.

I'm not talking about a scholar's minute technical formation, but the solid basis which can easily be gained from excellent and interesting books on theology and Scripture.

We don't need much, if we take well-suited and reliable texts, but we shouldn't read them like the evening paper or like a handbook on astronomy. We shouldn't whip through a chapter, feel that we've absorbed what it said, devour this book, the next book and find ourselves discontented without something new. There are books, very fine books with wonderful spiritual messages, which we can read like that (or almost), just for fun and for the companionship with genuinely holy people they provide. But I'm talking about something different.

Theology, for instance. A really good series like Schmaus' *Dogma*[8] can last us for years. If we need something lighter, we have a wonderful range available. We have to read this kind of thing with some continuity, not a page this week and a chapter a month later, but not necessarily every day. I only learned to study in the monastery.

First we must know what the author is saying. (!)

Then pick out the most important parts and the progression of thought.

Then find a way of remembering it. Note taking helps. Outlines too.

I've read wonderful books and forgotten what they said. One method I use now to get the meat out of a chapter is to make up a few questions, as if I were giving an exam. Then find the answers. It is much more fun than any method of study I've ever come across. A real game. How about making up your own courses and lesson plans? Be creative. Field trips. Cassettes.

But however we do it, we should relax and take our time. It

[8]Michael Schmaus, *Dogma*, (Sheed & Ward NY, 1968).

shouldn't be a chore but an adventure. When we pray, our knowledge shouldn't convert the prayer into intellectual speculation—marvelous shadowy castles of thought. The study should become a solid background, rescuing us from shallowness and sentimentality. In study, we are not trying to prove the faith to ourselves (or others). We are letting faith browse in green pastures, letting our minds feed on the truth for which they were made, entering into one field of our inheritance. We are intellectual beings as well as physical and emotional ones. Our minds need the truths of faith and the theological elaborations which God has provided.

A book like Romano Guardini's *The Lord*[9] is deeply theological, but more meditative and poetic than Schmaus. It demands slow meditative reading, and would not be patient of a study technique. It wants to be gone back to, as do any of these deeply rooted books.

Stay in the main line. Schmaus is very contemporary, yet solid.

Scripture: Here, I believe, we have no right to remain fundamentalists. Fundamentalism simply is not true, and only truth can be the legitimate food of the mind and heart. We will erect no bridges with our children by defending what is not true. And we do not need to fear the legitimate findings of modern scriptural scholarship. There is a very solid stream of scholarship which in no way endangers our faith but enlightens and enriches and is in perfect harmony with tradition. We have an obligation to study and absorb it, and this study can make Scripture a thousand times more exciting.

[9]Romano Guardini, *The Lord* (Henry Regnery, Chicago, 1954).

I started with Charlier's *A Christian Approach to the Bible*.[10] It is still a good and very interesting introduction.

To use a commentary for individual books: Don't be in a hurry. Start at the beginning. Make sure you have mastered the material in the introductory section, the basic themes of, say, Mark's Gospel. (Wilfrid Harrington's commentary is excellent and I like that whole series.[11] You might also like the Collegeville pamphlet.)[12] Then proceed section by section, with the biblical text, slowly stopping to pray and assimilate. Use the text of the Biblical commentary for *Lectio* during your prayer time. A commentary can irritate if you don't take your time, and you can wind up with a blur of half-remembered facts. This kind of reading is demanding but much more rewarding than a more facile type (which is also a good thing, merely different. An exciting, fast moving spiritual book can provide a sort of atmosphere which neutralizes the unfortunate aspects of parts of our culture. It can be like fresh air. It is just great that the Lord approaches us lovingly on every level).

If you're the creative sort, there are vast possibilities for projects to make this study more exciting. You can make wonderful notebooks in colored pens. Diagrams, pictures, plays. Tracing of themes. Comparisons of parallel passages in the Synoptics with the differences picked out to show the theological emphasis of each Evangelist. (Some of these suggestions come from Sisters taking a formal course.) A study and a

[10]Celestin Charlier, *A Christian Approach to the Bible* (Newman Press, Westminster MD 1959).

[11]*New Testament Message: Old Testament Message*, (Michael Glazier, Wilmington DE).

[12]*New Testament Reading Guide: Old Testament Reading Guide* (Liturgical Press, Collegeville MN).

celebration of the great Biblical symbols. Even create some exercises to develop sensitivity to symbolism in a culture which is oriented to the scientific and rational.

I fear that in what I've said about study I've made it sound dreary and hard. I don't want to because it is wonderful. This is the place for a marriage of our prayer with the natural exercise of our thinking and imaginative powers. It's something we're made for. And even the disorganized, falling-out-at-the-edges kind of thing I've been able to do in scraps of time has been such a help to me. I have never so appreciated the divinity as well as the humanity of Christ, and I could never have so appreciated his centrality without it.

Don't confuse study with spiritual reading. Study is a practical discipline. It exercises our managing faculties, and has its own part to play in the life of grace. It's worth the trouble. Our spiritual lives won't run on feelings, and it's nice to have something else around. We spend loads of time and money on education for a career. But we assume our religious life can get along without study. It doesn't make sense.

At the same time, I'm not saying we can't—or shouldn't—read the Bible without having a thorough knowledge of Scriptural studies, or that if we genuinely can't find time for a (sort of) organized type of study, we are out of luck. We do our best. Many books on a study list are fun. The methods of study I mentioned are interesting, at least for me. But the point is to learn in a way that's interesting for you. It won't help to make study so demanding and minute that you can't stand the drudgery and quit altogether.

## Spiritual Reading

Spiritual reading isn't a technical discipline like study, and different faculties are involved, a different attitude. It's not a getting-on-top of things, but a receptivity. We may use the same books we use for study. With this different approach, we may, for instance, take half an hour to absorb a few paragraphs or a few pages of Schmaus, or slowly read a text from *Mark* with its commentary. Or we may choose a meditative book which would be unsuitable for study, perhaps Eddie Doherty's *Psalms of a Sinner*.[13] We learn from this kind of book as well, and it should have a good theological foundation. But in either case, the purpose is not to master a body of material but to open oneself to God, be present to him, listen and enjoy him through the medium of what we absorb.

Either study or reading can become prayer. We can stop now and then and let it. The reading of course more easily will. But generally, these activities are not exactly prayer, but study or reading done in an atmosphere of prayer, and as themselves valuable. Just as meals and school and cleaning house and supporting one's family are valuable as what they are. We have to pay attention to what they demand of us, and we can make them into another *kind* of prayer by letting them be what they are meant to be.

And even the newspaper can be approached as background for prayer. We get the *Christian Science Monitor* and its competence gives me a big thrill—the kind I would get from a great play or book, a first-rate dancer or athlete—the thrill of fine craftsmanship. (One of my constant frustrations is not

[13]Edward Doherty, *Psalms of a Sinner* (Abbey Press, St. Meinrad IN).

being able to write letters to the editor. I would like to say how much I admire the paper, and to put in my two cents now and then. Even when I disagree with its presentation, it's with respect. Mostly I like the depth, the giving of a number of positions, and the confidence with which it addresses people as thoughtful and capable of reason, discussion, and solution.) But even *inferior* papers can give you—if you stop and think about it that way—an opportunity to root your prayer in God's saving will for the world. We must seek our little plot of solitude, but only so we can put out practical arms to the God who is moving and working in our whole universe.

Today I prayed before a picture of a basset hound puppy nuzzling its mother's chin. I have always wanted to see a basset hound puppy. I like their baggy legs and mournful faces and long silky ears. I would like one in heaven and I will name it Jeremiah. It takes an interesting God to make basset hounds. He couldn't possibly be stuffy. (The pups are like their mothers only rounder, proportionately, in the middle.)

# 4

# KEEPING THE LIKENESS

Now we will go on to the rest of the background. Or the rest of the Christian life. Except there are no precise divisions. It all interlaces and blends.

## Moral Effort

You could also say "the pursuit of virtue" or "character building". It all sounds Victorian and unpleasant. I've called it part of the background for prayer, but that is more false than true. The reason for this is that, together with prayer, it forms something else. Prayer is not the purpose of life. The purpose of life is a mystery, in the proper sense. We can never fully define it, we can only walk around it and describe it from different perspectives, hint, make analogies, This helps. But we mustn't think we know all about it.

You could call it surrender to God. You could call it integration of the person. Or restoration to the fullness of our destiny as image and likeness of God. Or participation in the paschal journey of Christ. Or total openness to the living Christ who is given us in Baptism. Or passage into the whole Christ. Or the return of the universe to its creative fullness. Or an infinite number of other things. I remember Fulton Sheen once giving a radio talk on human love and marriage. He ended, "If this is the spark, what must be the flame?" Whatever our destiny in terms of description, its reality is not stuffy. No human beauty can come near it, and the more deeply we appreciate it and move into it, the more deeply we know and appreciate the human beauties which mirror it and hold it in their own being. We can't begin to know creation until we have learned its source and its inner mystery to some small extent.

Moral effort isn't dreary, an unpleasant duty undertaken for the sake of a dim heavenly kingdom. It's not a way of strengthening our powers so that we will have the capacity to resist sin and thus live respectable, constructive, moral lives out of the center of which we can know ourselves approved by God. It isn't fixing ourselves up to be pleasing to God. We aren't making ourselves good enough for God.

We don't start in the center of our goodness. We don't even start on the beginning of a road toward that goodness. We start in the center (if we may use the term) of God. It's as if we were a nut in a shell which has been tossed into the shoreless ocean of God. The shell has to be cracked or eroded or worn away or battered away because it separates us from his love. God's love is always there. It doesn't depend on our goodness, but on his nature. He couldn't stop loving us without changing his nature, which is to be love.

Or we could say that we are born within walls, and the purpose of life is to let them be battered down, carried off stone by stone, so that his tender and glorious love may come pouring into every cranny of our being.

Or, to shift metaphors, *again*, God has put himself entirely into our hands, and the work of our life is to realize this and give ourselves in return. Or we are like something fragmented and dispersed, without a center or any active force to bring us into harmony; and God has breathed into us such a force, a dynamism which will gather our scattered pieces and make us whole. Our entire being is in the process of such a whole-ing and our life of virtue is a loving surrender to his creative work. The important point in all of this is that we begin with the gift. We begin with this mysterious whole-ing force within, reaching out to embrace every faculty. We have been given to. Our life is a reaching out in gratitude to embrace the gift.

## Self-Knowledge

The life of virtue needs self-knowledge. We can't (for instance) correct a habit of critical thought and speech, of constant whiney complaint or of constant self-display without knowing a) that we do it, b) why we get such a kick out of it, and c) what would be the best means of dealing with it.

Self-knowledge has other advantages. It brings with it the

gift of understanding the human psyche and, consequently, of compassion. Once I have experienced my own weakness, faced it, chased it down to the roots, and tried to do something about it, I will be battered and sobered and not immediately anxious to feel superior to someone else. Even better, we understand the whys of someone else, and learn how to reach another to help, support, and heal. We really can't love deeply until we have reached the place in ourselves where we share the absolute neediness of all humankind.

But it brings an even greater benefit. It is here, on this level, that we confront the fabrication we have made of ourselves, the great thing we have always had to be. It may be no dramatic experience, it may be an over-and-over very ordinary experience. Yet here, confronting our unwillingness to be and to be known simply as this person loved by God, this need filled with his beneficent gentleness, we begin to be able to love him. We are asked to accept who we are and journey as Frodo did, leaving various pots and pans and armor behind.[14] We come by this door to a real instead of an intellectual knowledge of what mercy is—one way of experiencing the jubilant and inrushing joy of God's love for us. It is at this point that our walls start cracking and we begin really to know the intensity of Christ's death and resurrection in ourselves. Unfortunately (or fortunately) this is only a beginning.

How do we get self-knowledge? Here, as always, we shouldn't try to force God's hand, to do a good job on ourselves so as to take care of the whole business and present ourselves for his approval. A gift is a gift. A very simple method will do:

[14]J.R.R. Tolkien, The Lord of the Rings (Houghton Mifflin, NY 1965).

1) Tell the Lord simply and sincerely that you want to be told about the areas in yourself which are resisting him. Be very frank and tell him you would rather be comfortable, you would rather choose your own asceticism (or leave it alone), that you are afraid he'll choose something painful, but you realize this is the way to love, and you are game to try. Then live your life, praying and trying as you have been to be happy, kind, and responsible. Don't go digging and raking inside. If you keep trying to see Jesus in every event of your life, and praise him gently and in a relaxed way, he will take care of the gift of self-knowledge. There is nothing that shows us up more clearly than the radiant presence of the Lord.

2) Someday a quite ordinary circumstance will give you light. You will tread somebody down in conversation, and the thought will come, "Do I always do this? Am I more interested in my own ideas than in anyone else's? Am I straining at the bit until that bore gets finished?" Check if you can with a good friend "Is this really me?" But don't go to someone for a complete catalog of your faults. He might be wrong; you couldn't handle it if he were right. We have to proceed a little at a time.

3) Be faithful in trying to moderate the objectionable thing gently and with good humor. Your fidelity will draw down more light. (Remember, keep asking.) You will have enough self-knowledge to grow on. The Lord is faithful if we keep our eyes on him. We needn't and shouldn't grow introspective.

While we're on the subject, here is a good method for dealing with what's wrong with you: If you only see one fault, use that—it's all very simple. If you see many, try to decide which is the more radical (not the more obvious). By this I mean the one which tends to cause the others. Maybe you need a little help from a friend or brother or sister. But good will is all that's necessary, even a good guess. You don't need a psychological examination. The branches lead eventually to the root. The main thing is to concentrate on one. Another good criterion for the best candidate is that it be something you can work on with fair frequency. If you lose your temper twice a month, you're better off working on not doing everything in a rush. The temper will be affected sooner or later. If you can find a trustworthy spiritual director to help in the project, you've got a prize.

The key words in the "working on," are concrete practicality, moderation, consistency, and faith:

## Practicality

Choose *one* very concrete practice which you can exercise a reasonable number of times in the day. If you have a fiercely competitive nature and *must* win or come out somewhere at the top or be miserable, it is probably part of a complex personality structure. But you don't need an intricate analysis. The concrete way of beginning is to choose one manifestation of this aggressiveness—say, "I deliver my opinions like infallible pronouncements. I am less interested in truth, courtesy and learning from others than in displaying that I am right." Since people do a lot of talking in the normal course of life, the field for improvement is broad. The practice can be something like "I will make one conversation a day into an acted prayer. I will create a small private vestibule as it begins, then during it I will watch gently for the Lord as he comes to me in other people, or the other person. I will try to draw the others out, and provide a receptive, creative atmosphere in which they can be themselves. I will not become wallpaper, but channel my energy into creating a communion of humor, exchange, relaxation, search. The whole, the bringing together of all of us in a loving union of recreation or serious discussion will be my aim, not to wind the conversation around myself as if it were decoration on the main feature. At the end, I will thank you whether I did well or not, praise you whether I forgot or not. I will make a simple inward motion of sharing with you."

## Consistency

Our practice must be practical in order to be consistent. Not a big spectacular push on Saturday when I happen to feel like it, and nothing at all on Monday when I want to enjoy my grouch. Not big efforts when I see results and half-hearted ones when I have little success. Steady, consistent, faithful, gentle effort. *Moderation* relates to this: if we choose an extreme, something mentally or physically overloading, we can't be consistent. We'll lag when we get strained and tired. We'll also be in danger of drawing attention to ourselves. The idea about virtue is that it should be unobtrusive — not a little stool on which we climb to be admired. There are lots of stories about desert Fathers who lost their virtues when they left communities to become hermits. They no longer had an audience, and moral effort became unbearably burdensome.

## Faith

This is not *your* project. It is God's. It is God's. It needs prayer and it needs the relaxed attitude of someone who leaves the results in God's hands, content with the privilege of trying. We are not forcing our virtue on God. He has no obligation to make it turn out as we wish. We are giving *ourselves* to him in this particular form, not demanding of him that he make of us what we want. It is, as the older terminology put it, a supernatural proposition. We are not using God as an instrument in our self-improvement scheme. We are not forcing him into making of us something we will get a kick out of being.

## Picking up Pieces

To return a moment to the example above. What we do is try to see a broader picture. Not just our one obviously superior opinion. What we don't do is try to repress our God-given personality, cease contributing to conversations, for instance, or adopt an artificial attitude (making ourselves a respectable pain in the neck), or try to be like so-and-so. We also keep in mind that there are times to talk a lot, times to just let go with a friend and pour out what we're like inside at that particular moment. The idea is not to sacrifice your spontaneity but to enlighten it with a more complete understanding of the needs of others and an appreciation of what they can give you if you don't prevent them. You put your genuine self at the service of others; you don't make up a self for the purpose.

Another example: Say I have a considerable emotional investment in trifles. I fly off the handle over every little annoyance. This also may be part of a larger pattern, but I can start with what I see. The best plan is not: "I will not get mad at anyone today." You've got all that emotion just waiting to be stepped on, and you will not succeed. Once maybe. Twice. But by then you're twice as tense, and your reaction will be twice as strong when you *do* let go. Then you will get discouraged and stop trying. Then you will feel you're not good enough for God, become angry at him for not helping you to become good enough to please him, find prayer more and more difficult and quit altogether.

It is better to say, "Whenever I encounter an annoyance today, big or small, I will praise God with an act of faith that somehow, in a way hidden to me, this little contradiction has another side which will be something beautiful for me. I will try to picture Jesus working out a great gift for me in this small incident. If I've already gotten annoyed, I will praise him for the annoying thing and for my weakness. I will ask him to release in me his healing love and understanding." That way, whether or not you "succeed," you have released the power of God into the situation, even into its shambles, and you have begun where you should—at your vision of faith.

The hardest thing in the practice of virtue is to redeem a failed attempt. You've already lost your temper, or passed on that piece of gossip or thrashed around in critical judgments— and you remember that this particular area was your practice, and now you've gone and blown it.

We have a strong incentive when we begin anything. It's new and it has endless possibilities and we picture ourselves as successful. If we do manage to bring the thing off fairly well, we have added incentive to continue and finish off with a flourish—we are pleased with ourselves, and that carries us on. But when we're in the middle of a self-made mess, or licking our wounds in the wreckage afterwards, we want only to forget the whole business, walk off, and—if this isn't the 90th time and we aren't totally discouraged—find a new start tomorrow and the possibility of doing *really well*.

The point here is a) that there is no better or deeper act of virtue we can perform than in picking up pieces in the midst of a little project that we have messed up, and b) the reason we are so upset is because we wanted success for ourselves rather than giving God his response. When he lets us stub our noses, we resent him for not catering to our sense of being good and therefore deserving of his love.

What can I do? If, in the midst of a flare-up, I can catch myself, and accepting that I have already made a fool of myself, simmer down and agree to lose the face I am willing to defend in even this last ditch, I can praise God for showing me how much I need him, for wanting me to share even this failure with him. I can open my wounded self to him and thank him for loving me so much that even this is a gift he very much desires to have. And this, even if I didn't catch myself in time to backtrack with my victim.

If we demanded that all our acts of virtue be successes, we would never get anywhere, and we would become tyrants over God. It is the daily sincere trying and the picking up of many pieces that draws us into a realized intimacy with him.

If you say that this will encourage a slovenly attitude in the first place, "I'll let that guy have it and then pick up the pieces afterwards," first try the picking-up—even once is uncomfortable and deep enough to make you really prefer not to have to do it—consistently. Accept, confront your responsibility "*I* did this. *My* habitual attitude toward life is responsible." And then place this in God's hands, sharing your hurt pride, letting him show you that maybe you care more about your failure than about the hurt you caused. Let him peel off a few layers of defensiveness. Realize that the person who stood there and worked no miracle to save you from yourself has done it with tenderness, and the hand which wields the scalpel of self-knowledge is giving you a gift, that he welcomes you into his arms as you open up a few more inches of your defended depths. See that he loves you so intensely that he *must* enter you this way; it is the only way you will open to him. He must prevent your virtue from becoming a defense against yielding to him, letting him come personally deep deep into you.

It won't provide you with an excuse for giving somebody else a rough time. The more you realize how much God accepts you in this way, how every incident, every going-to-him is a deepening of his relationship with you, the more you will *want* to seek him in occurrences which were only irritants before.

## 5

# CONSTRUCTIVE FAILURE

There is no way to avoid the uncomfortable aspects of self-knowledge and of failure. We should not court them, digging endlessly within ourselves, agonizing over faults. But we can't grow without some pain. This pain has to be talked about when we discuss a life of prayer. It's useless to give methods and guidelines unless we are ready to talk about an area which can kill all desire for prayer.

The more faithful you are to prayer, the more aware you will become of what is not good in you. The more you work at virtue, the more experience you will have of failure. Yet you still must relate to God.

I used to wonder what difference the Redemption made,

since I was still so selfish and disintegrated. For all I could see, I might just as well have remained in Original Sin. Why was Paul so enthusiastic about Redemption? "We are at peace with God." How? Every day was a struggle. I was very much helped in this by Schmaus.[15] He discusses the primary element of Original Sin:

> Original Sin means that man is enclosed in himself and cannot, owing to his weakness and his incapacity for love and commitment, break through the walls of his self-imprisonment...Only if God in the initiative of his creative love breaks into this self-enclosure and thus opens the way to true freedom can a change take place. As the result of Original Sin, God must make his breakthrough anew in each man: he makes it at any given moment in the Christ event. Christ has brought a new epoch into being, yet it must be actualized for each individual personally if it is to exert its saving effects on him.
>
> The condition of man in Original Sin, then, can be described as an 'incapacity for dialog.' With respect to its personal element, Original Sin consists in the lack of desire and capacity for dialog with God, and consequently for loving and altruistic (and not simply aimless) dialog with one's fellow man. It is the incapacity for being a genuine partner. Because he is without the bond with Jesus, the Man for others, man is content in his inability to make contact with others, in his arrogant and self-seeking isolation. He is dominated by the power of sin.

The definition we learned—that Original Sin is the lack of that holiness and justice (sanctifying grace) which man should possess—is true but has to be situated in the context of the primary, personal element which he describes above.

[15]Schmaus, Vol. II.

After awhile, I began to see unredeemed man as disjointed, his life spinning away from him, his faculties lost in a perpetually centrifugal movement, with no center, no power to pull them together. The redemptive love of God has set Christ within us as our center. He permeates all our faculties and sets them on their journey home—to that center of ourself which he was always meant to be. We are saved and made holy in a radical way.

For his own reasons, he has not done this so as to spare us the struggle of the journey. We must labor at putting ourselves together, feel the pain and weariness of every part plodding back to its center. There are so many reasons why he has not done "a better job." One is that if we had got to heaven without having shared Christ's passion and death in our own members, we would be disappointed. There would be a way in which we could have shared his life, and we'd have missed out on it. If you love someone terrribly, you want to share all you can of him.

Another is that there will be a particular joy for us in knowing that we have been totally loved every step of the way, that even unredeemed man is totally loved. There is security in knowing we are loved for who we are, and not for the sake of our goodness. No sin can cause the loss of God's love or its diminution. (If we turn away from God, choose to sin and not return, we discard our relationship, we bar him out. But we bar out a lover.) Forever we will have the joy of knowing that he loved us in this way.

I labor this because we can't embrace a serious spiritual life without experiencing—some people more than others—the confusion and pain of feeling shut away from God by our inadequacy. The person who sets out with an ingrained sense of inadequacy feels it most, but even the ebullient extrovert will feel it to some degree. It is then that we have to realize that the struggle itself, the prosaic, modest keeping-at-it, the daily prayer, the daily work on our one practice is what counts to God. This is where "I am the way" (the road) really fits. The way is what God wants, the relationship which grows out of our ups and downs. He's not out for the kind of perfection we want. He's out for the love, the faith, the sharing, the trust, the picking up of pieces, the coming back. This often painful, flop-ful journey is a big love story and he wants it with all his heart.

If he let us become perfect specimens, we would soon forget to need him, we would grow our walls again. It is more important for us to taste our helpessness than to be interminably good. He wants all the moments of reconciliation every step of the way.

*We* feel our failure to measure up to what *we* have determined he must want in order to be pleased with us. In faith, we must drop this image of the perfect me, not in despair and sulks. We mustn't drop the holy road of incredible intimacy with God because it is his idea of what he wants, not ours. We must keep walking it on his terms.

Every faculty of ours is alive with the life of the Risen Lord. It is straining toward its center. We are used to thinking of Jesus as the revelation of God to men, and this is true. But he is also the revelation of man, and the perfect answer of man to God. In him the everlasting yearning of God for man and of man for God is satisfied. And it is our destiny to share in this perfect embrace. We are not on our own. To be on our own is to be trapped within impenetrable walls. This common, ordinary, often discouraging but faithful (well, generally faithful) journey of ours is much more than ours. It is the constant rhythm of Jesus' death and resurrection. We are really planted in the likeness of his death and come up like the spikes of those tulips that stick their heads out of the tomb like little happy flags in April. Most of the time we aren't as pleased with life as we should be, because we don't realize the value of a life which shows us so often its ordinary side, its wanting side. The smallest act of kindness is an infinite celebration because it is Christ dying and rising from the dead.

And if we feel, as we often may, separated from God, unworthy of God, and if we experience him as crushingly other, Jesus also felt that, emotionally. He shared to the full our emotional alienation from God. It can often be helpful at these times to place ourselves within his own sense of rejection and desolation. He loved us enough to share even this with us. And now our pain is a sharing in his. It is not hopeless and sterile but the touch of an intense love, the place of profound sharing.

We can surely sin, but sin itself no longer has the character it had in an unredeemed life. It is caught up sooner or later in the movement which is now placed as a dynamism in every faculty of our being and becomes part of the stream which bears us Godward, which thrusts us deeper and deeper into the center of who we really are.

### Contrition

I haven't even mentioned contrition. Contrition comes from a word meaning broken. Compunction, which is an abiding sense of contrition, comes from a word meaning to put a hole in—puncture. To us, contrition can cause a problem, and an abiding sense of contrition can be very unattractive.

One Ash Wednesday, it occurred to me that the purpose of the whole business was contrition, and I felt I should make some formal acknowledgement of this. But I realized that to do so, to say "I'm sorry" for a most undistinguished and largely self-centered existence, would be not only false but almost an expression of rebellion.

Instead, I said something like this: Lord, I am supposed to be sorry, but I'm not. I'm not sorry for the mediocrity of my life and for my sins and offenses against you. They hurt me more than they hurt you. I *want* to be good. I work hard at it. In fact you know that I want to be perfect so that I will be pleased with myself and have the power within myself to control your attitude and the attitude of everyone else toward me. To be sinful, to be in danger of acting selfishly or flaring up at threat to my sense of self leaves me in the insecurity of having to rely on your love instead of on a power in my own control. My offenses against you and against others are some of the most painful experiences of my life because they seem to remove me from love. They are in consequence some of the costliest gifts I have to offer you. Certainly I'm sorry for them, but for all the wrong reasons. Could it be that what is asked of me now is not to ask your forgiveness, but to ask you to let *me* forgive *you*? Will you help me forgive you for leaving me a human being instead of a machine?

I think it is much harder to forgive God for our sins—for letting us remain weak and short-sighted and short-tempered—than to ask his forgiveness for them. Trying to forgive him can be very dredging, and get up into sight a lot of hidden resentment. We can go along making acts of contrition, feeling all the while that it's unfair—it's *his* fault. Or that constant apologizing is something we would never do in a good human friendship. We can feel that God wants more than we can give, and that to be in a constant state of regret is nobody's idea of relationship.

This emotional response is partially because we don't understand *why* he leaves us faulty. And maybe one way of summarizing what I've been saying is to say that he wants of us the special, faith-ed kind of love that only this situation can bring.

But another reason for our feeling this way is that we don't understand the nature of God's love and the nature of contrition. (We respond emotionally according to human experience, and often even with the clearest sort of understanding, our emotions can still go their own way. But if we keep choosing according to truth and not according to those feelings which are not emerging from truth, the emotions are laid open to God in trust and simple sharing, and they too become an instrument of intimacy.)

This passage from Schmaus[16] on God's changeless love fits in very well:

> Ever since the creation of the world God has been directed towards the creature according to his changeless will : he is

[16]Schmaus, Vol. II.

continuously engaged in giving himself to the creature. It is on the creature's side that the question arises: how God fares with man—whether he is received at all, whether the creature opens up to him. The receptivity of the creature to the divine love was most intense in Jesus Christ and in his acts of obedience which were summed up on the cross. Therefore God could give himself to Christ, dying on the cross, with the power which demonstrated its salvific dynamism in the resurrection. Because Jesus Christ was the representative of mankind, God gave himself to all mankind in giving himself to Christ. By means of the cross mankind was reconciled to God. Augustine's words are most apposite here: "When *you* change, *he* changes."

Man does not change God's mind by means of his religious acts; rather, he himself becomes capable of accepting God's gifts. In prayer, especially in the supplication which is an undertone in every prayer, man confesses his limitations, his weaknesses, his sinfulness. Supplication does not become a means whereby man gains power over God, or magic through which he puts God at his disposal. Instead it is an instrument in God's hands putting man at his disposal in the sense that it permits him to give himself to man.

If we remember what we said about contrition as a breaking, and compunction as a piercing, then contrition becomes part of a large and wonderful picture. It isn't the formal act which must follow each offense tidily in order to secure forgiveness. It isn't the placating of someone easily offended. It's the constant state (compunction) of taking our finger out of the dike, of letting our walls be broken, our shell punctured. Our sins, great and small, as well as what we call imperfections, are much more than "things," like blocks of wood, to be destroyed by forgiveness. Yes, we were wrong. But our sins are also symptoms of a basic interior attitude, one of refusing to let

God give himself to us. Contrition as an habitual state, and also as a celebration of self-giving (on our part and his) at particular times, is a vast element in the dance of our salvation. It is faith opening the barred doors and the arms wrapped around ourselves, so that we can embrace the love which has never ceased beating on those doors and waiting for our arms to be free.

I once complained that "obedience" was a totally inadequate word for the reality it was meant to signify, and I was put in my place by being told that its derivation makes it mean "to listen." By contrition we turn back our whole selves from deafness to listening, we let ourselves be placed back in the obedience of Christ and in the eternal embrace of God and man which is his saving death and resurrection.

It's really not a question of "If God is a pushover, why not do what I want and fix it up later?" His commandments aren't arbitrary. They are sign posts warning us lest we violate our own natures and hurt ourselves. The more we give in to patterns of wrong, the deeper its ruts become in us, and the harder it is to open up and to begin new patterns of grace.

But for redeemed man, even his sin is turned into a blessing, even his headstrong self-will. Compunction lets in a healing love which does not just erase sin but transforms it into glorious other things. It becomes first of all the occasion of the piercing of our shell, then realization of our true need of God. It grows into wisdom, understanding, self-knowledge, compassion, maturity. To nurse it with remorse, to refuse to accept ourselves as the person who has sinned, to refuse God forgiveness and actually to refuse his forgiveness of us is to keep putting plaster on the broken areas of our wall. It's refusing to accept the wonderful transforming power of God's love. Eugene Boylan, OCSO, used to say that many people who became great saints could never have ended that way had they not sinned seriously somewhere along the line. They learned their need. Go out and sin? No. God has other ways. But those who have hard things to remember should always remember them wrapped tightly in God's transforming tenderness. They are, translucent with contrition and with grace, glorious holy places where he meets us in intimate gift.

In actuality, the person who has not got himself into a pattern of serious sin will realize sooner or later that his journey isn't all that different. He sees in himself the underlying attitude which would have become sin had God not stood in the way. He also realizes that "being good," remaining on this side of the commandments, while useful to society, is not of itself a particularly dynamic state. One can be good for many wrong reasons. One can be good for reasons which themselves stand in the way of yielding oneself to God.

There is even a state of declaring yourself the greatest of all sinners. To which my abbess says drily, "Well, if you aren't getting much attention, that's one way of giving it to yourself."

A very nice little prayer method, which kind of sums up the heart of our Christian effort is this: Sit with your hands tightly knotted into fists and laid on your lap. Very slowly and gently, open one finger at a time, starting with one hand, then passing to the next. Leave your fingers loose and relaxed, not stiffly out straight. Breathe slowly and deeply. Leave your hands open on your lap. simply being conscious of your bodily position. You can, after awhile go on to the Jesus prayer or a word-prayer. Or you can use this as a superb act of contrition.

Or a quick way of being present and given in a tight situation. Or a vestibule to any kind of acted prayer. Or almost anything you can think of. Before a crucifix. Thanksgiving for a beautiful gift of someone's love.

Going to bed at night is a symbol of eternal sleep, or the consummation of our love story with God. "Night prayers" can be perfunctions; or very brief ones can be very meaningful. Of course you would like to wipe the slate clean, but I have found that big sweeping generalities are never as real or helpful as a single very concrete thing. To forgive everyone who has ever hurt you, to be sorry for every sin and for the attitude underneath, to sweep your whole spiritual horizon with one whop of the broom seems a little unreal to me. There may be times when the Spirit pushes us to this, times when it's appropriate. But for most of us, I shouldn't think often.

It is better to recall one concrete incident of the day in which we failed, and open it gently to the healing power of God. Then perhaps lift out of memory someone who has hurt us and left wounds which still haven't healed, and ask God to flood the aching area with his own forgiveness. Then forgive him for the thing which we most regret in this day or which most hurt us. Even just *one* of these would be a good night prayer, and then dunking ourselves into the Paschal mystery within, to go to sleep in it. Also do not fail to read *God Speaks* for Peguy's marvelous insight into sleep.[17]

Another excellent thing is to lift out of the day one grace, one success or picking-up-of-pieces, one perfectly beautiful moment and share it with God in gratitude. We are not nearly

[17]Charles Peguy, tr. Julian Green, *God Speaks* (Pantheon NY, 1945).

grateful enough for the moral goodness in us which we take for granted. If we are not prostitutes or drug addicts or alchoholics or living with somebody else's husband, it is because we have been kept in the palm of his hand.

And although I'm not qualified to say much about it, maybe I could stick in a reminder that the sexual union of a married couple is sacramental, priestly and prayer. Marriage would be a natural sacrament even if it had not received churchly consecration. All the sacraments flow from and draw us back into the death and resurrection of Christ. Sexual love is participation in the total giving of Christ.

I have thoughts on the subject, but I dislike reading the opinions of people who have no experience in what they're talking about. People who want to may work it out—but in the realistic context of imperfect human life, and imperfect human marriages.

# 6

# THE CHEERFUL ASCETIC

By asceticism, I mean the patterns of action which we undertake in order to become more free of domination by needs and drives, more flexible to the Spirit, more controlled and so able to give.

It is a difficult subject because we are chained in different ways and to different things. We can make ends of our ascetical practices and wind up with ascetical practices instead of love. Control becomes a reinforcement of the wall keeping God out. Instead of surrender we cultivate self-mastery. Control, instead of a tool with which we can answer God's demands, becomes a form of independence.

## Fasting

I hate to say to people who live in a comfortable culture, "Don't fast." But I do want to discuss it. It has some advantages:

So many of our brothers in the world are dying of hunger. Fasting is a way of reaching out to them, especially when we contribute to their welfare out of what we have saved. It can be an assertion of spiritual and moral values in a time and place where these have yielded to material values. It can be a reminder to myself that control is possible when a moral temptation is very pressing. It can be a way of communing with the spiritual presence already in the world, drawing matter and the work of man's hands into a higher fulfilment.

An extended experience of fasting (Lent) can give us an understanding of our own weakness. When we have been short-tempered and soggy from physical pressure, when our religious fervor has been effectively short-circuited by the effects of an exterior situation, we're likely to be more compassionate of the falls of others, less cocky in our own moments of pious enthusiasm. We can understand more clearly that our fervor can arise out of physical well-being and our religious lassitude out of self-deflation, and consequently put less confidence in how we feel about things.

However, fasting is psychologically complex. In this part of the discussion, I'm talking about fasting as a deprivation of some part of the normal amount of food necessary to maintain us in physical and psychological well-being—we make ourselves uncomfortable by eating less than our bodies normally require.

Before I entered the monastery, I fasted for Lent. It was from choice, and I didn't have much company. I was "doing something" for Lent. It was uncomfortable but satisfying. By Holy Saturday, I had accomplished something. When I came to the monastery, I'm sure the *amount* of food available during Lent was not less, but the psychological situation was very different. I wasn't distinctive; everyone did the same. Lent was a long, long, bleak stretch of depression, fatigue, scratchy temper, and resentment at having to go through it at all. Before, my body had fasted while my vanity was fed. Now my vanity suffered and so my body was not sustained in its fast. (Presently, the regulation is less stringent, and I'm supposed to take milk between meals so Lent is a snap.) I've never forgotten this. Fasting is not good *in itself*, and can become a form of self-affirmation. The "being different" part can even take on a group aspect. The understanding which grows between Christians who are sharing a deepening experience of life is legitimate and helpful. But like anything else, it is open to a counterfeit. We can sustain our ascetic efforts on the ego-trip of belonging. We are part of a group, a set, a sort of elite. We do different "things."

Another, even more serious difficulty is present in the idea of a votive fast. I ask God for something and I fast in the pursuit of that request. Or I am preparing myself for something—the painting of an icon, the writing of an article—and fast in order to do the thing with less selfishness, more openness to the spiritual reality I am trying to convey. For many people, the rationale behind this is confused, and even when it isn't, a danger is present. The legitimate justification for this fast is that when I ask something of God, I want to show that I love enough to sacrifice my comfort for the person from whom I ask it. I want to enter the sufferings of Christ, from which all grace flows, be as close as possible to the Paschal Mystery. If it is done in preparation for a sacred act, I want to disengage myself from what may be a too-clinging attitude toward the material world in order to come closer to the Spirit and thus help to reconsecrate by means of the Spirit the material world in which God moves and speaks.

The trouble is that very quickly, and sometimes sub-consciously, I begin to view the matter as a kind of barter, *quid pro quo*. So much discomfort equals so much grace. Or, because I am fasting I somehow *oblige* God to answer my question, inspire my effort, help my friend. Or, God will not give an answer unless it is wrested out of him by some affliction. And often I come to feel that the really important things to God are the painful ones. The extreme case of this mentality is feeling as if God were some kind of banker handling transactions in human pain. Even the redemptive action of Christ comes to be viewed that way. I've forgotten the whole gift character of our relationship with God, and that the very word grace means pure, undeserved gift. It's consoling and beautiful to know that our pain can help others. But in this barter mentality, we've got the context all wrong.

There is also the previously mentioned danger that fasting becomes something I have to do because my sense of self is involved with the image of someone who fasts. I can be very ascetic and still be unaware of character faults which are grinding down the nerves of other people and obstructing my relationships with them and with God.

Which means two things: One is that no human effort is

free of the possibility (and the actuality) of self-interest. We can't take any ascetical practice for granted. It has to be integrated with discretion into our entire love story with God. The other flows from this—a need for simple, practical guidelines.

These are the guidelines I would suggest if you really think you should fast:

1. Don't go beyond the Church fast (Only fluids between meals, one full meal with two others which together do not equal a full meal. Meat only at the main meal—*if* this is possible without making a display of yourself.) Don't fast on fruit juice for 24 hours, for instance.
2. If your health is precarious, find some other practice. It'll help your humility.
3. Be unobtrusive and don't make yourself a pain in the neck to others. Be ready to ditch the fast if charity indicates it.
4. Don't let yourself get hooked on the importance of fasting, and make sure it's not interfering with more important elements—even obligations—of your spiritual life.
5. Be prudent in the amount of fasting you do.
6. Fasting is meant to be undertaken in the context of a sensible eating pattern. If your eating habits are unbalanced and unhealthful in one way or another, your fasting is irrational. You cannot isolate fasting from the whole picture and call it virtuous. The balance of the whole determines whether the fast is virtue or self-indulgence.

There is another form of asceticism with regard to food, which is demanding and very low-key. You could call it a responsible attitude toward food:

Is my eating pattern really healthful, or do I pick at junk all day?

If I ate properly at meals, could I go without solid food between meals?

Are my meals always taken in a rush to get somewhere else?

Am I willing to eat what I don't like, or eat something healthful instead of something which I like or which does me no good?

When I'm responsible for the family meals, do I take the responsibility seriously or do other things come first, things which really shouldn't and don't have to?

Could I make meal preparation a more interesting and creative project for myself and my family?

Am I sufficiently aware of the sacramental character of meals? Should I do a little research on the symbolism, and could I do more to make them acted prayers? (Not by talking holy.) Do meals contribute to the creation of the family or are they things to get done so everyone can get on with something more interesting?

There's more to it, I'm sure. Often it should be, if possible, a family project. Just don't get a divorce over it.

## Other Things

When it comes to other forms of ascetical practice, I am still happy with the low-key, well-integrated moderate approach.

A consistent, moderate approach to anything over the long haul is bound to be helpful. Remember, you undertake anything for the purpose of making yourself supple to God (rather, letting him make you so), not for the purpose of spiritual athletics. The things that go deep inside and change you at that point where you are stuck on your own opinions, compulsions, self-exaltation, self-will, self-defense, are what really help.

Someday a book should be written entitled A *Happy Handbook of Ascetic Practice.*

A few things like this should go into it.

Fields ripe for harvest:

## 1. CURIOSITY

Is my curiosity a positive good? Do I utilize it in the pursuit of truth and the uncovering of the beauty God has put into his world? It is possible to be mentally lazy when my vocation is asking me to work a little harder at digging, speculating. Maybe the tone of my recreational interests could be enriched by research on any number of fabulous topics. Do I need all that TV or would something else be more healthful and ultimately relaxing? Am I responsible to my curiosity as a faculty God-given for my benefit, as an indication of the Spirit's desire to make me happier, richer, more helpful to others?

In what ways does a negative surrender to curiosity harm my spiritual and mental health? Do I grab for a paper or magazine the moment its interesting headline meets my eye? Or can I wait an hour, a day? Can I put away a letter for a few hours, a day? And then make it a real communion, a beautiful moment, a prayer?

How am I in respect to someone else's privacy? How much time goes into minding someone else's business? Can I tactfully change the conversation when it gets gossipy?

Am I dominated by the need to indulge my curiosities? Can I back off and evaluate before satisfying myself? Are there some things—maybe a lot of things—I take in which only clutter my life and make prayer difficult? What is the quality of the stuff I feed my mind on? How much time do I waste on low-grade stuff?


## 2. LIFE STYLE


This is tricky because sometimes a family or group is involved, and we have to search together for solutions, which for many reasons, are not ideal, but only better. However, even their partial quality can be helpful, and the fact that they are unable (because of circumstances beyond our control) to be other than partial is also in itself a benefit. We aren't able to set up our world for ourselves and must lie flexibly on the surface of the sea like C.S. Lewis' islands.[18] Our virtue can't get in God's way.

Jean LeClerq has indicated that the primary contemporary form of asceticism is selectivity. We are surrounded by too much of everything, a lot of it catchy and of low-quality,

[18]C.S. Lewis, *Perelandra* (MacMillan, 1944).

much of it valuable and good. We not only have to come to decisions on what wrong things to leave out, we have to decide what good things to leave out. If we flit from one interest to another, making of ourselves small vacant lots on which everything going by can be tossed, we'll never be able to go deeply into anything.

Getting space for our daily prayer time is a supremely necessary asceticism. No good to say "But I pray all day." The quality of your daily communion with God, as well as your ability to find him in the movement of daily events grows out of the time you are willing to throw away on an often boring and seemingly unproductive effort at a daily prayer period. Then you weigh other interests against a prudent, balanced effort at some study time and spiritual reading time. Even ten minutes is a help. Remember that it will ultimately be a gift to your family.

All sorts of questions pop up. What kind of music do I want to spend my time on? What place should TV have, and what *kind* of TV? Will a long-term educational project require the sacrifice of other things I enjoy and should I plan for this?

Do I spend enough time with my family, or am I restless to get away and get something done? Is my family life a real being—present, a communion with them in the Lord? Do I know how to *enjoy*? Am I willing to take time to learn? Am I able to take pleasure out of small common things?

How am I with the outdoors? Can I let myself relax with it and take on its rhythm? Can I be quiet with it as well as active? Do I just use it as a backdrop to sports or do I let it enter me and moderate my desire to dominate? Can I be humble before it?

How am I on wasting material goods? Do I make conservation into a prayer?

Am I letting events and passing enthusiasms form my life, or is there a goal, a core of values and needs at the center, giving me a life in which God will be the integrating thread?

## 3.RESPONSIBILITY FOR MY VIEWS

Yes, I am free to hold views which attract me. I am also responsible for them.

Are my views habitually emotions with a plaster of rationalization on top? Am I tense and miserable at the expression of contradictory views? Do I try to examine objective bases for important issues? Do I waste newspaper-reading time on gossip sections and flamboyant events when I should be trying to understand really important issues in depth? Can I have a discussion, in distinction to a polite (or not so polite) exposition of my infallible views?

Am I so impressionable that I have no convictions? Or so inflexible that nothing could make me change my mind? Can I continue to love people who differ with me on emotional issues?

I have to say here that emotional involvement is complex. I can identify with something very good, very deserving of defense. The only trouble is that when I have a high emotional stake in the cause, the cause (very naturally) becomes me, and then the cause (also very naturally) disappears in the me without my realizing it. This is where prayer is very necessary, and good doses of self-knowledge. When the defense of the good becomes an orgy of self-assertion, I can harm the cause as well as myself. Yes, I have to defend the good, but I have to know how to go about it in the right way.

Also, and I have to be honest about this, there are times when a moral statement is not required of us, and our emotional identification with an issue is so intense that we have to keep quiet. We can tell the Lord, and sometimes even the friends who are in danger of getting in the line of fire, that we wish very much we didn't feel this way, but as things stand, we are disqualified from the discussion. We can even unite our silence with that of Christ, and make it a prayer. Above all, we should not let the emotion separate us from him. (If I were really *good*, this wouldn't happen. He knows how I feel about so-and-so and her miserable way of looking at things.) Let him in. Maybe he agrees with you. At any rate, don't go away from him until you can come back with a party face. He doesn't *want* the party face. He wants *you*, right now. Don't throw away your suffering because you're ashamed of it. Let him take it and see what he can do with it.

## 4. CULTURE

Have I decided it's too much trouble to gain an appreciation of art, history, better books?

## 5. SMALL HABITS

Do I have small irritating habits that cause annoyance to others?

Throat clearing, coughing, picking at nails. Having to readjust any object on the table just a little bit. Having to have an area around myself in which small things must go the way I want them, and requiring other people to adjust.

Dominating every discussion. Or never contributing until it is dragged out of me.


## 6. LARGE HABIT

Anyone who wants to quit (or not start) smoking is doing a very good thing.

A list like this is not meant to be a checklist. (Have I done all this? What do I do next? How long will it take?) It's suggestions from which we can choose. It's also a way of indicating ascetic possibilities which open doors and unclench fists and make it a little easier to say yes. The principles involved:

One's state of life comes first. Our ascetical practice should be in harmony with the demands of our state of life—whether student or wife or whatever. It should help make us a better student or a more humane investor or a better integrated scientist and father.

It should be a game of love, not an athletic contest.

It should harmonize with our main effort at moral reform (Remember, way back there?) That is the essential ascetic effort, with which everything else should harmonize.

It should make us easier to live with.

It should be limited and consistent.

All the practices since we got off deprivation of food are really not too subject to the dangers mentioned for fasting, and fasting without this other type of asceticism is kind of silly. You can always declare a fast on curiosity, or declare for yourself a few hours of total relaxed presence to those who live on your love. A fast on gossip? Or having to be right? Or always being in a rush?

Or a fast on noise. Do I always need sound? The radio on in the car? Can I actually find some pockets of quiet in the day—and leave them alone? Do I have the courage to be quiet, to face silence? To *make* some? To make some within when the outside is noisy?

Obviously, a lot of this overlaps the moral effort, because the moral effort is an ascetic practice in itself, a method of giving ourselves to healing.

The greatest instrument of moral effort, as well as ascetical practice, to my mind, is exemplified in Rev. Carothers' life of praise. It harmonizes with an attitude of loving surrender, and allows God to work on us. Our best organized efforts can only say to God, as Hubert Van Zeller puts it, "I don't seem to be doing very well at giving. Please come and take." And to set it in the context of a life of praise decreases an enormous amount of complication. The method of praise can be misunderstood, but not after it's been really lived. Objections I've heard come under two heads. "Praise God for something awful? For cancer? For war?" Of course not. Praise him for the loving power within these tragedies, which somehow in this world or the next, will turn them inside out so that we can see the beauty of a resolution which now is hidden from us. A resolution which is connected with our confidence in his power to bring it about. Remember the children in the snowstorm? They walked right over the place they most wanted to be in. Another objection is, "Praise God so he'll remove the painful situation? Praise as a mechanism to squeeze relief out of God?" Not at all. Praise as a way of letting God change *us*. Praise as an expression of faith. The circumstances may or may not alter, but we will. Praise is simply a way of putting to work our gift of faith, and faith is what Christianity is about.

One of my friends says that she only recommends this method to people who are in their last ditch, because it is such a complete form of abandonment that usually people won't let God take such radical charge of their lives until they have no other choice.

# 7

# THE CRAFT OF APPRECIATION

How to cope with what is wrong in someone else is one of the basic steps in personal relationship. I don't pretend to have easy answers, but I can share a few observations. ("A few"—if you haven't already drowned in observations.)

There are faults and faults. There are also mere personality traits, but I'm not talking about that.

Some faults the person knows about, works at, and feels badly about still having.

Some faults can't be faced, or can't yet be faced by the person. He needs support until he can grow some more.

Some are temporary growing pains.

Some are patient of correction if they're known. The person asks for help, wants to know.

Some are pretty nearly beyond help. The person can only be loved.

Some are obvious to everybody. The person would be happier in the long run if he knew, even though he's not asking.

Whether it's prudent to say something (and sometimes it's the courageous thing, and for parents and often brothers and sisters and close friends, a real responsibility, providing it's done in a prudent way), we have still to live with and love faulty people. Our life of prayer and our spotty success with our own moral effort is going to help our undertaking. Some other insights also may be useful:

We should not regard others' faults as "Today would be OK if it weren't for X and his arrogance (small-mindedness/criticism/snobbery/ambition)." Faults are not misfortunes in the way of an abundant life. One of the greatest tests of maturity is our ability to integrate into our lives the world's (and our own) imperfection.

The faults of which someone is aware, or will become aware, are usually left by God for some good purpose in view of that person's growth. He needs humility more than he needs to be perfect. These are sometimes much more painful to him than to us. (Moodiness, for instance. Or the humiliating failure to conquer a quick temper. Anger is really painful to the person getting mad.)

The faults people don't see, or can't see, the faults no one else can help them with are a mystery we must pray to enter. Our own helplessness is a door into the helplessness of Christ as he stood before a humanity which refused him entrance. And we have no notion at all of why we can see something of our own need, while someone else cannot. Our *seeing* is a responsibility. It may well be that we are less as a person than he, because he has, for some reason, not incurred the responsibility.

Hubert Van Zeller has a good story about a novice who was charged with taking a very cantankerous old Sister on her daily stroll in a wheelchair. The old woman was so demanding, so mean and belligerent and unable to be satisfied, that the younger sister hated the job and hated *her*. One day she was pushing the chair on a downward slope toward the pond. As the complaints went on, she began to push faster, until the chair was rocketing toward the water and looked to be ending up in a cold dive. Just on the brink, she wrenched it back and her own body jerked forward until she saw in the water the reflection of her own face and that of her charge. The old woman's face was beautiful, as radiant as an angel's, her own was hideous, distorted and deformed.

We can be sure that in any encounter with another's weakness, we are not stumbling on an error in the universe, but a very holy place in which God is present and working. Our negative attitude can impede his work. Our loving acceptance of the mystery can help. The fault may be left for the good of the other or for *ours*.

Sometimes we can only praise God for the person, try to be supportive and understanding. We must realize, for instance, that it is very hard for someone with a low self-image to be humble. The self-image is an open wound. When we do have responsibility for helping someone see the problem, that is an opportunity for a different kind of understanding. Often, being willing to share our own weakness is a help. The other will not then feel threatened by a superior person. Or introducing a difficult person to prayer and praise. Often there's a serious psychological complex underneath. A person can't just determine to be more agreeable. Time is needed. And if God is taking more time than we like, it's because the other's rough edges are needed by *us*.

In our efforts to be understanding, we must sometimes have the charity not to give in, not to reinforce a negative behaviour patterns, but still to remain open, loving, and kind. For instance, the dictator who has everything his own way by dint of bad temper. (Although in some situations, one is really helpless with this type.) Understanding must be loving enough to be firm.

There remains the person whose faults cause me the most exasperation, struggle, and pain—*me*. We do our best, we let our weakness draw us into a loving relationship with God, we don't give up. Yet ultimately, one of the greatest prayers—and sometimes the hardest—is the acceptance of myself just as I am.

## Criticism

In the area we've been examining would fall an attitude of virtue which spans every category and evidences both spiritual and mental health. Everything I've said so far would sound familiar to my community, since it's a reflection of the formation with which we have been gifted. But this particular element of our formation is one for which I am uniquely grateful. I could call it the art of dealing with our critical faculties.

We live in a world of criticism. The first reaction, the ultimate reaction to everything is criticism. It ranges from the perpetual whine to the sophisticated superiority of an educated condemnation, from chronic protest to small personal digs. For many people, it is an entire identity.

We also live in a world where a lot is open to criticism. We can't accept the evaporation of moral standards, violation of human rights, racism, exploitation of the poor and environment, the abortion racket, the nuclear mess—the list goes on. We're responsible citizens of a democracy, and this requires of us that we be alert and well informed and ready to do something when a moral issue is at stake.

In a talk given during one of her congressional campaigns, Margaret Heckler referred to a prayer breakfast she had attended in Washington. "All the people sitting at the tables were white, and all the people serving were black. Those people were reading the Bible, but they weren't living it."

If we then distinguish between our objects of criticism, placing on one side moral and socially-moral issues, together with questions of policy (the most efficient or practical or possible ways of getting good things done), and on the other side the rest of our gripes and pickings-apart, I wonder what we would find.

*Even when its object is legitimate:*

How much of my criticism is necessary and constructive? Does it serve any good end?

What about the motivation behind it? Do I criticize legitimate targets for the sake of feeling superior, for the sake of being witty?

Have I a sufficiently mature appreciation of the difficulties involved in the project under my scalpel, and am I aware that it's a rare project which hasn't got its share of compromise, error, insufficiency?

What is the manner of my objections? I love the *Monitor* for its Christian courtesy. It seems to believe that rational presentations of facts and principles can be the most powerful force for sustaining good and working against evil. Not everyone would agree. But I question the personal judgments, the violence, the back and front hand rancor of media presentation. I hear very little of it and when I do, it strikes me keenly. When President Reagan was shot, I was interested in the rudeness of the reporters. They were in a tough spot, but they were reacting with violence. We complain when somebody shoots the president, yet our commonest habits are violent. The criticism of President Carter often attacked less his policies than his person, both directly and obliquely. Our criticism is violent in form.[19]

*If its object is not legitimate:*

I hurt myself so much. Criticism is corrosive of the personality. I shut off endless possiblities for praising God in faith. I choose to see what I don't like; therefore I can't see God moving quietly to bring the situation into glory.

I hurt others. If in no other way, by withdrawing my spiritual support. I block the channels in myself through which God means his life and help to reach them.

There is nothing more destructive of our relationship with God.

Criticism of any kind is a managing faculty. It dissects, evaluates. Even its periods of appreciation are evaluative. This

[19]See Paul Tournier, *The Violence Within* (Harper and Row NY, 1978).

has its place, but that place should not be disproportionate. We should not spend all our time standing over above or over against the world. We should spend as much time as possible in wonder and appreciation, looking up.

And when the criticism is emotionally based, the complaint which reinforces my sense of importance, it isn't even a rational process. I am eating my brother to make myself fat.

Once I dipped into an article in *The Catholic Worker*. I always start from the back, and I didn't know who had written it. It was so vitriolic, I was unhappy with it, then saddened to see it was by Dan Berrigan. So I thought, he is preaching pacifism in a violent frame of mind. I believe he is sincere, but I also know you can't be a genuine pacifist, or genuinely helpful, through violence of the mind any more than through violence of the body. I never had that impression with Dorothy Day. She was terribly convinced, terribly dedicated. But she was interiorly calm. She had humor, she could see that other people would usually think she was nuts, but she didn't attack them emotionally for disagreeing. She was dry, extreme, loving, reverent— a very disarming anarchist, someone in whom protest had not become an identity. I am glad I didn't have her vocation, for it's a rare person who could do what she did, and with such inner freedom.

Above all, we must not judge someone's interior. We can't understand the complicated motivations in someone else's heart. You see this imputed motivation in the media constantly. It would be a rather depressing game to underline it in articles or pick it out on the radio.

I pass this on, not to sermonize, but because I have come to see it as one of the foundation stones of the life in Christ. We can't stuff up all the channels into (and out of) our hearts, and still live in him. We can't let ourselves measure the world by emotional drives within ourselves which we don't even understand.

One of Rabbi Heschel's beautiful statements fits here: "Every hour is unique and the only one given at the moment, exclusive and endlessly precious."[20] We can only fully (well, never *fully*, but at least more fully) understand anyone or anything after we have loved it, stood before it without condemnation, quietly and respectfully. The love may be hard, even a tragic love, but if I cut what is before me into slices for the satisfaction of what is least in me, I have not known it, and I have not given to the world the saving love which God could have poured out through me. Anything I criticise comes into me and is digested by me. It is never any bigger than I, and a world I treat this way will never be any bigger than the smallest of me. I will not grow up to the world and it will not grow because of me.

I realize this isn't fashionable, but I have to give it as the fruit of my experience. I grew up as a critical person. To grow out of it has been a great gift. It's not that one doesn't *see*, but that one is able to see more.

This fits in with Jean LeClerq's remark about selectivity. The unjustified clutter-type of criticism has no constructive end, and it hurts me even more than its object. The constant seeing of what I deplore has also to go. It's a matter of selectivity. Just what, out of all that bothers me, can I do something constructive about, and just what are my responsibilities?

[20]Abraham J. Heschel, *The Sabbath* (Farrar, Straus and Giroux NY, 1951).

Finding out can be fun. It can also be fun to drop the load of complaint about things I can't help, fun to create a light and appreciative atmosphere in which others can grow. Where to start? Right now. Right here.

I know. Right now and right here are always wrong. They offer no opportunities and everyone is awful. Fine. But there's no place else to start. If we don't want to strangle in our own criticism for the rest of our lives, let's look around.

Are complaints littering my head so badly that there is no room for God, no room for joy? Is what I could do to improve the world smothering in my anger at what I can't possibly change? My primary responsibilities, my prayer, my love for others -have they soured while I carp over disagreeable magazine articles, while I pour my own disappointments, my sense of being unloved, into criticism of others? Or of the world in general?

Again, am I *sure* I complain about the right things? And if I do, where is someone who can give me something real to do about them? We have a friend who helps out the Kampuchean new-comers to East Providence. And I mean *helps*. People like that make the world less desperate and they can find things for us to do which are tailored to fit into the pattern of our prior responsibilities. We can't enter every possible good project, and this itself is the asceticism of selectivity. We're doing it for others, also, to help them put their feet on a road they can walk with assurance. We're not using it to boost the sense of being a social hero.

How about my family relationships? Can someone help me to help, instead of adding discomfort to discomfort? My friendships? Are my friends all mirrors of me? Same ethnic background, same tastes, same interests? Can't I build new bridges out of shared pleasures? If I'm into new studies, perhaps a new friend or two would make the project more interesting—especially if it's someone who needs a boost.

Complaint can take the form of tension. When I'm doing all I can, I feel obliged to worry about every project I'm involved in as well as everything I can't help out with. As if the worry accomplished what my hands can't. As if I had to torment myself with guilt over everything I can't heal, as if the whole world depended on me. So I make my own area of the world that much more miserable—me, my family and friends, my bus driver. Even the mailman doesn't want to meet me at the door. This is not quite the idea of a social conscience.

The difference between just working and working in faith is something like this: If I can bring myself to leave a few things to God, if I can will to see him working quietly even in difficulties that upset me, and if I can accept that he has what it takes to bring them to an harmonious resolution while my back is turned—then my praise helps me to become an instrument of genuine healing even in wounded areas my hands cannot reach.

This would also be an answer for those who have to say, "But even with two jobs, the money doesn't stretch, and I never see my kids. I can't do any more." Or, "I'm a single parent with a full time job. I haven't time for the the friends I have now." God doesn't want any more doing from you then. If you really want to do more, how about this? For every critical thought you catch, substitute a quick prayer of praise for the person or circumstance bothering you, and the broken world and everyone who seems not to care. By the end of the day, you'll have done as much for the improvement of what you wanted to criticize as if you'd had an active hand in righting every wrong.

If you're in a position like this, you may be critical because you're tired and you know you're going to be tired world without end. You may get angry with your wife because she's happy in her job and you aren't. Just recognizing the emotional forces behind your criticism and bringing them honestly to God in prayer can go a long way toward lessening your own allotment of the world's distress. More often than we care to acknowledge, criticism is the voice of an emotional disability. Outward circumstances may be pressing against our feelings—overwork, a failing marriage: The boss would be a colorful and entertaining character if I weren't carrying a load of guilt over my daughter's drug problem.

Or we may have a chronic emotional disorder: I wouldn't get so mad at the pope or the postal service if I hadn't learned to expect failure in every project I put my hand to (and maybe I wouldn't fail so much if I had gotten encouragement instead of criticism myself). I could get along with authority if every authority situation did not rake my sense of inferiority.

This is one of the advantages of admitting to ourselves that our habits of criticism are not really evidences of a superior analytical mind, but attitudes that can hurt us very much. We'll be able to see deeper into ourselves, find the roots of this thing we no longer admire in ourselves. Usually we'll realize we need help—possibly just a friend to be open with. We will find that either we can't stop criticising (like alcohol: "Oh I could stop if I wanted to, any time." Try.) or if we do, the emotional forces beneath will find another outlet.

Two of my married friends, both well-balanced, exceptionally gifted women, could not survive the stresses of ordinary life without each other to call every day. They are blessed with an unusually beautiful friendship. Sometimes we need a clergyman, sometimes a professional counselor. Always we have the prayer of emotional honesty. God can take everything we have to dump on him and more.

Adrian Van Kaam, CSSp, has written many excellent books. I was recently reading *Spirituality and the Gentle Life*,[21] which is very fine. Written for us who live in a culture marked by violence, it discloses hidden forms of violence in the personality, and shows us how to avoid being drawn into currents of violence which we have not recognized. But the author would not want us to use his presentation as an excuse for demanding of life all the circumstances necessary for perfect calm. Certainly we should not cultivate a violent life-style, and we should try to receive gently such roughness as we are dealt. But life cannot always be gentle to us, and we need time to learn how to be gentle to it. Life has often all the gentleness of a bargain basement, and it is well for us that it does. We must become detached even from our own gentleness.

Be careful with that word "detachment". One chapter title in this book includes the words "the death of desire." Read the chapter, don't just say, "Ick", and walk away. Detachment doesn't mean not loving, it means loving well. We love if we learn, little by little, not to use another as an instrument for getting-my-own-way. I love the natural world by relating to it with respect and courtesy. I love both people and things by

[21]Adrian Van Kaam, CSSp, *Spirituality and the Gentle Life* (Dimension Books, Denville NJ, 1974).

leaving about them an area of peace and space in which they can be themselves, without forcing and cutting them into my own shape and size. It's not our desires that are wrong. It's the way in which we let them mold our personalities that can be wrong. If they emerge as genuine expressions of love, they are part of our life in God. If they harmonize with our greatest love, they will not cause us the wrenching anxieties and disappointments that come with being torn by every attraction. Or if we must suffer from them, we will have peace deep down, knowing we are struggling in grace, and this is one step along the road.

So we should not read a word like "detachment" and think of an emotionless robot. Any more than a word like "gentle" should make us think of spineless fish and wet washcloths. Gentleness is strength and energy expressing itself in understanding, respect, and other-centeredness. All kinds of people can be gentle—the forceful, dynamic, creative, enthusiastic person is perfected in this expression of love—not doused. Not making the satisfaction of all my desires the center of the world, and leaving space in which people can move about in an area of respect, does not of course mean we don't form our children or contribute creatively to the growth of a friend. Firmness is not the opposite of gentleness. Firmness is a form of gentleness, even when it hurts. Violence is the opposite of gentleness, and violence has more forms than IRA bombings and hunger strikes. For instance, constant rush, ill manners, want of understanding, *having* to win or be first or maintain a position of exclusive prominence in an area I have staked out for myself, argument which seeks not to grow but to prevail. To be indulgent to a child, even a grown-up child, in a way which deprives the other of character isn't gentle.

# 8

## MOPPINGS-UP

I should end on an inspiring note, but I am all "wrote-out".

What if nothing works? Well, our *plans* usually don't, but his love always finds a corner to sneak around. He devises our route, with bends and shortcuts and endless long cuts. We must not mind that what we conceive of as the end remains so unattainable. He is the end, and he is always here. Our simple ways of approach or of realizing his presence always "work", whether they satisfy us or not. Often we have to invite him into a personal junk pile of extensive proportions, but he is glad. It was there all along, wanting him, but we were afraid to notice.

With regard to prayer itself, when we have done what we

can, and the prayer is difficult and unsatisfactory, we must keep putting in the time. To take the time away from our work, our interesting pursuits, our making of the world, and give it away to God, put it out of our management is itself a prayer. (By this I don't mean never prepare or use a simple framework or provide background.) And the helplessness which comes after we have done our part is somehow necessary. Often, help comes at other times than prayer, *because* we have sacrificed our own satisfaction at prayertime.

But there's more to it, and more to the question of why our hurts interfere with what we conceive of as prayer, and why they cause disturbances in our intellectual appreciation of God and his ways. Or even why we don't have tangible evidences, "experiences" of God.

An experience of God (according to the popular notion of an experience) can often be given to someone who could not find God any other way. They are signposts on the way to faith for people who would otherwise get lost. But they are not themselves faith, and faith is the real thing.

Our beginning level of faith is a beginning. When people say "I can't *do* anything!" not without resentment and beating of fists against closed doors, they can be getting beyond the beginning. The real stuff takes place down where we are done to and given to. Down beyond the managing efforts of even the best and most useful ego. And it takes place often in the midst of and in harmony with (and at the expense of—ugh) ego efforts (ego in the good sense) which God obviously wants. Sometimes the ego is laboring and getting nowhere at its holy activities and it's killing us. That's OK. The real work goes on underneath.

I think no one but God could possibly appreciate his crazy sense of order. When he's in charge, the people who love organization never seem to get organized. As I said in the beginning, we could all "pray" better if our nerve ends were not exposed to rejection or the conviction of it, unemployment, too much employment, failure, opposition, grief. But God does not want us in charge. He can take much better care of us than we can. We might as well let him.

At this point I could stick in a couple more humble ways of making prayer out of the ordinary—even when nothing works. You will develop others on your own.

One peaceful way of praying is presence to our surroundings. If you are outside under a tree, look up at the pattern of leaves as the sun makes them dark or light. Look gently at a single flower (sometimes the ones as big as a little fingernail are amazing), one leaf, a tree trunk, the lines of a house. Absorb, be present to the presence of God which it is, the beauty of God which it holds. Rain. The time of day (morning and midafternoon have entirely different characters). Ever sit in the presence of geranium leaves? They dance without moving. They were made as a dance. Or patterns of sunlight on a wall, or even of machinery.

I have found that a little hunk of time into which I want only to stuff a distraction of some kind is often the thing God seems to appreciate most. Impossible to concentrate, no "refreshment" that I can feel, not much time. Except that I stopped running long enough to love him consciously and to give him a very small present.

The whole point is simplicity. Our spiritual and moral life has to be woven harmoniously into our daily love, not become a complicated, wearisome burden carried on top of everything else. It should *help* us with our daily life, not make it worse.

## Answering Questions

We don't have to answer everything for other people. Often, all we can say is "Come and see." The reason for having faith (or the reason for justifying our living by faith) is the life itself—not extraordinary experiences but a different kind of experience along the long haul. It has to be lived. The person who says, "OK, I'll try," will find out. The one who goes away won't know, however long you talk. (Or not at least until God turns up on a bend of the path that seemed to lead straight away from him.)

There are advantages to the coming and seeing:

For one thing, we find deliverance from many personal knots, things which would otherwise bind us all our lives. Sometimes we have to hurt, but everybody has to, and you don't hurt worse because you're given to God. The hurt only becomes a road instead of a dead end. We can be delivered from wants which aren't wants, for really satisfying things, things worthy of being loved. We can be freed from narrowness of vision, to love and understand people.

Looking back, even when tired and hurting, you wouldn't change it for anything. You're becoming real. And whether you're a helpful person or a social disaster, just by what you are, you are of help to others.

The confusion that comes from living, and from putting that living up against our faith and saying "Why?" is just as instinctive a reaction, just—you might say—as superficial, as getting measles when you're exposed at the right age. You get muddled on the surface, but down where you can't understand, the real work is going on. Our minds scream for understanding. They were made for it. When they're frustrated, they react, they want their proper food. The trouble is, their proper food isn't the things they're grabbing for— rational, comforting explanations on a human level. Their proper food is the mystery of God, and he lets them squeal and thrash and muddle while he's quietly taking care of things underneath. Sooner or later they will simmer down and realize they are at home in the dark and really only contented there. They will cling and grasp and raise a ruckus for the goods of a more superficial kind not quite so consistently, of if they do continue, we will be able to pat them on the head and not mind so much, knowing they are only cases of measles after all.

And the joy is so much greater. Not something you keep digging for, but little flashes now and then, and also the sense of meaning and worth even when and if you *feel* meaningless.

I don't mean by this we can throw over the study. No good saying, "If it's going to break down somewhere, what the heck. I'll just enjoy my darkness." You have to go as far as you can. But you can't walk off with a blockbuster like the problem of evil tucked neatly under your arm. I promise, you will not come to any understanding of this until you stop trying to dominate it with your mind. And even then the help will not be direct, but diagonal.

"I have to teach. I have to know." Do you really think people want all the answers? *We* want all the answers so we can protect ourselves from God (I'm OK, you don't have to interfere, Lord), and so we can solve everybody else's problems. So we don't have to sit there in receptive silence when they pour their distress into our laps. We're like the TV commentators—keep talking. But I have seen suffering people, not once but many times, resent the comforters who seem to have it all together. "How can they know what it's like to be me?"

Sometimes our drive to understand attaches itself to the devil. He's an explanation. Personally, if I have to blame someone, I'd rather blame God, because then at least we've got a dialog going. A dialog with the devil is not profitable, and he gets too much attention that way. Pretty soon we wind up dominated by a devil who is so inflated he takes up all the room in the world, and God becomes a little shrunken thing for want of space. Just because we couldn't let go and live in mystery, because we had to get it all figured out, we've made a God nobody could like.

Let go of what you so desperately want to know. Your heart's in it and you hurt. But you can't understand until you stop trying. That kind of knowledge has to be given, and your mental muscles are so cramped they can't open up to receive. Let God tell you in his own time, in his own way. He will.

# AFTERWORD

Seen from the end, this attempt to gather a number of basic spiritual facts together in one place looks like a species of handbook. A lot has obviously been left out, and some of what got in has been said more than once. It was felt that the casual character of the piece should be retained, and it is now hoped that readers of what must have seemed more a letter than a book didn't mind hearing things over again. There is much I didn't say. I would like to start over: I'm tidy. But if there is one thing I know I said more than once, it's that life is now. We have to cultivate the art of making the best of it, and try to see the point of as many of its jokes as we can.

I did not say anything about common prayer or about its liturgical form. This is not because I don't expect anyone to go to church. For one thing, the people I was writing for came from a variety of religious traditions, and perhaps its present readers do too. For another, I think it's better to begin with individual spirituality and let the common prayer take care of itself as best it can. Until it begins to draw on the resources made available by personal prayer and moral effort. Then common and private prayer will have a chance to enrich each other. One can always devote spiritual reading and study time to liturgical texts in preparation, or to helpful books on the subject.

Actually, I'm not very good at it myself. Maybe this qualifies me to write about it some day, since someone who has trouble with anything may understand others who share the same trouble, and they may be able to struggle through together more effectively than if an expert had been called in to resolve the difficulty. A friend tells me her children always looked forward to the Sunday Eucharist. The Kiss of Peace was the high water mark of their week. Its object was to give one's brother such a bone-crushing hand clasp that he writhed under the strength of one's fraternal charity—unless he had the better grip. At the beginning of Mass, fellow-parishioners used to dash for the pews behind them for the entertainment value. There were only two parents to intersperse among seven children, and she has never found a book that was much help to her liturgical life.

Over another omission, I've been dallying to the last minute. I briefly mentioned the assistance of a spiritual director. It is obvious that we can be much helped by a competent director, a person of practical common sense whose chief value lies in not being us. We need the perspective of someone who is not in our skin, and who can in consequence say, "No, you do not need what you think you do. You need this much more humble thing instead." A director is not an excuse for long and frequent introspective conversations, a plumping—up of one's spiritual image, or the fine-tuning of some intricate mechanism of prayer. The director is there to encourage, to supply us with the honesty we need from a position outside ourselves. This kind of friend is so invaluable that I would like to say, "Please knock on the door of a rectory or manse or office. Or look for a wise married woman—in the Protestant tradition, a minister's wife is expected to have her share in the ministry—a Sister, someone in your field of work who has been living a dedicated single life."

And yet I have no idea who is behind that door. Will the man or woman be simple, practical, encouraging, and moderate? Or someone who will do more harm than good? I have no fear of the one to whom you feel like saying, "Oh, you don't understand. You can't be right. I'm much more spiritual than that." I would be afraid of matching a rigid director with a nervous person, or a permissive one with someone who needs a firm advisor. I would be afraid of some of the authors whose books I haven't pursued beyond a few pages, of extremists on either end. Or someone without a sense of humor. At any rate, be prudent. Ask around. Be simple, and I hope you're lucky. If the relationship puts you under tension, or the advice sounds peculiar, talk it over with someone whose common sense you respect. Don't be trapped into a genuinely unsuitable situation.

Another area which I did not explore is one which has a

special interest for me. In this book I have used the phrase "the love of God" as something which is attractive and reassuring, or at least possible. There are some people for whom it is not. I want someday to write for them.